Together Again:

Reconstituting God's Body

John C' de Baca

Copyright © 2014 John C' de Baca.

All rights reserved. No part of this book may be used or reproduced by any means, graphic, electronic, or mechanical, including photocopying, recording, taping or by any information storage retrieval system without the written permission of the publisher except in the case of brief quotations embodied in critical articles and reviews.

All New Testament quotations are the author's translation taken from The Greek New Testament, Third Edition, United Bible Societies, 1983

WestBow Press books may be ordered through booksellers or by contacting:

WestBow Press
A Division of Thomas Nelson & Zondervan
1663 Liberty Drive
Bloomington, IN 47403
www.westbowpress.com
1 (866) 928-1240

Because of the dynamic nature of the Internet, any web addresses or links contained in this book may have changed since publication and may no longer be valid. The views expressed in this work are solely those of the author and do not necessarily reflect the views of the publisher, and the publisher hereby disclaims any responsibility for them.

Any people depicted in stock imagery provided by Thinkstock are models, and such images are being used for illustrative purposes only.
Certain stock imagery © Thinkstock.

ISBN: 978-1-4908-2989-0 (sc)
ISBN: 978-1-4908-2990-6 (hc)
ISBN: 978-1-4908-2988-3 (e)

Library of Congress Control Number: 2014904807

Printed in the United States of America.

WestBow Press rev. date: 03/27/2014

CONTENTS

Introduction vii
1. The Metamorphosis of God 1
   In the Beginning Was the Word 1
   God's Real Presence in the Creation 24
   Preparing for Christ 35
2. A Beginning with Promise 44
   From God's Bleeding Side 44
   Pictures that Point 51
   The Big Picture 65
3. The Sinner on the Cross 77
   No Substitute Was Crucified 77
   Crucified With Christ 99
   How It Really Happens 116
4. Truths and Falsehoods about Hell 128
   A Question of Reality 128
   The Illogic of It 132
   The Truth of It 138
   Eternal Worms, and Other Oddities 149
5. A Mathematical Mistake 159
   Three Equals One, They Say 159
   Other Passages and True Interpretations 170
   The Exaltation of the Saints 179
   A Changing God 184
6. The Gospel of Glory 190
   God's Loving Call 190

"If I speak the truth, why do you not believe me?"
(John 8:46)

INTRODUCTION

Much of bedrock Christian doctrine and tradition is actually at variance with the Bible message. Unwittingly, the churches of Christianity have apostatized. Their central doctrines are bursting with blasphemies that malign God and dishonor Jesus even while they believe that they worship in truth.

But they should have known better. This apostasy was foreshadowed by Israel's history. That tragic and shameful history was itself a prophecy. Christianity is an echo of Israel. But the echo will be much louder than the original. The foreshadowings will be fulfilled in an even more shameful and tragic manner by Israel's younger sister. True to form, she who takes pride in being the "new Israel" has unswervingly followed the idolatrous path forged by her foreshadowing prototype. Shockingly, in their apostasy the churches of Christianity have substituted an idol for the living God. Satan walks openly among them, unrecognized. The God of most Christian churches is a fiendish gargoyle, baptized to give it legitimacy, and clothed fashionably with false doctrines that hide its true nature.

This present work points an incriminating finger at the well-hidden and unrecognized idolatries of today's new Israel. Perhaps a remnant of true believers will open their eyes. In any event, a warning will have been sounded.

It should be read with an open Bible at hand, preferably next to a table while seated, because its truth will pull the rug right out from under anyone standing on orthodoxy or tradition. It will be an earthquake in the minds of zealous Bible believers. So be careful.

Chapter **ONE**

The Metamorphosis of God

In the Beginning Was the Word

The churches of Christianity don't realize they are holding a monstrosity in their arms. Warmed by his closeness, with their eyes closed dreamily in his tight embrace, they feel safe and secure. But the God of their dreams is an idol of unrecognized blasphemies and infinite evil. He is not the loving God of the Bible.

Across the long centuries, a heavy accumulation of erroneous traditions has been thrown over God's self-portrait. Christian doctrine has become a thick, blanketing shroud hanging heavily over the cross. Those grave-clothes of tradition must be pulled off and thrown away. God's glory must be allowed to shine forth again openly. But sadly, loyalty always stands guard over tradition. To get rid of tradition, you must first get past loyalty.

Believers are programmed. In every church, loyalty to their own tradition is pushed as a virtue. It's called faith, and the people are urged to be faithful. The mantra is, "trust and obey." Loyalty to tradition is equated with loyalty to Christ and the truth, and easily becomes the love of their spiritual lives. And when zeal is added to loyalty and tradition, it trumps reason every time. Indeed, reason sometimes is viewed as the antithesis of faith.

All the churches have their loyalists, quick to the defense of their dogma. In every church, traditionalists are convinced that they possess the God-given truths of the Bible, to be guarded with zeal and steadfastness, no matter their biblical support. After all, those dogmas have impressive pedigrees. They come with long histories from trusted and respected leaders. Criticism of a church's dogma doesn't just reproach today's faithful, then. It's also a reproach against their forbears, against the founders of their tradition, the heroes of their faith. In traditionalist eyes criticism can become a rash and foolish rejection of history and of truth itself. And so in every church the various hand-me-down doctrines are unthinkingly followed, blasphemous though they may be. Loyalty to tradition keeps the shroud of errors firmly in place, draped securely over the cross.

On the other hand, many of the attendees who warm the pews in this post-modern world, as well as those who don't, just don't care, one way or another. The common attitude is that your set of beliefs is as good as mine. Or maybe mine's better, but let's not fuss over it. Religion is a private matter. To each his own. Truth is relative, after all, and no one has a monopoly on it. Peace is what matters. Let's not disturb the peace. Live and let live. Why fuss about doctrine? Let's learn to get along together.

This nonchalance and apathy over doctrine is the shoe on the other foot. Both shoes have fallen. This has led to an easy acceptance of strange and irrational doctrines that cannot stand close scrutiny. Loyalty and apathy, religion and secularism, both keep the traditions firmly in place. If the truth is to be seen clearly, the traditions must be torn away.

One of these traditions waves God off into a separate world, high and away in utter holiness, far above the dirt and grime that ever clings to embodiedness. He is pure Spirit, they claim, a Holy Ghost, ephemeral and other-worldly. And strangely, he has three heads. Well, strangely, he has three heads and he doesn't have three heads. The churches have substituted an incomprehensible three-headed gargoyle with only one head for the living God of Scripture. But because their gargoyle is a Spirit rather than wood or stone, said to live in the Bible and in their heart, they think to have avoided the trap of idolatry. So they strive hard to please him in their lives and in their worship. They strive for a close personal relationship with him.

But substitution, wherever found, is always false. Always. That's a strong statement, but it's valid and true. To substitute is to make believe that one thing is another. That's not possible, child. And yet this silly game of pretend is played passionately every week in the churches. It's pure fiction. Substitution is a lie candy coated to mask its taste so it will go down easier. But eat too much of it and you'll get sick.

And that's what has happened. The churches have swallowed too much substitution and have become feverish. They've lost touch with reality. A substitute for God, even if it's spirit, even if it's made of doctrines and traditions instead of wood or stone, is an idol. Setting it up in church doesn't make it real. And a substitute Christ is actually an Antichrist. But unfortunately, substitution is now central to Christian doctrine.

Christianity donned these bright clothes of pretense and make-believe early, and the people still wear them every Sunday. In churches of every stripe, the faithful take great care not to soil these Sunday clothes of make-believe by questioning or doubting. The people are persuaded that true faith upholds their beliefs. They must "trust and obey." So, in every church there stands a golden calf with three heads which are supposedly one head. It's a substitute God made up of impossible lies and unrecognized blasphemies. There it stands, motionless and immutable, robed with error, while the leaders proudly cry out, "Here is your God, O Israel." And they eagerly and passionately present this substitute god, this golden gargoyle, to the people for worship. Incredible? No, child, it's happening everywhere. The churches of Christianity have apostatized. They've fallen into appallingly false traditions. And they don't recognize how foolish and blasphemous is their worship.

Because their idol is spiritual rather than physical, because it's made of words put together into sweet-tasting, candy-coated doctrines that make them feel good, they don't recognize it as an idol. Instead, they draw it tightly to their breast and sing its praises. Thinking to honor God, they flatter their idol to the high heavens. He is pure Spirit, they claim, and untouched by the dirt and grime that clings to the things of this world.

The shroud of false traditions must be removed. How? Will it come off with a polite tug, if we smile and say nice, feely-touchy things? No, it's heavy. And it's stuck. We must yank on it vigorously, repeatedly. So, that's what we'll do. Let the traditionalists huff and puff. Forget politeness. We'll be frank and blunt, and in your face. We'll yank the shroud vigorously aside. Let the dust fly. It will be worth the effort. The truth will be seen, again.

God's Original Embodiedness

We can begin with the nontraditional and disquieting idea that God once was embodied. Yes, in the beginning, at the creation, God had a body. The disquieting truth of his embodiedness has always been there, but it was hidden under the shroud. Now, upon seeing it suddenly for the first time it may shock and awe traditionalists, like a ghost that unexpectedly materializes and speaks. But is it a ghost, or is it an angel? Either way, ghost or angel, the truth of God's embodiedness will challenge most churchmen cushioned comfortably in the overstuffed chairs of tradition and orthodoxy. Yes, the biblical record presents the disturbing truth that God was embodied when our world was formed. In the beginning, God had a body. In the beginning, the divine Body and the divine Spirit were One.

Believe it, child. Wrap your brain around the idea. Hug it tightly, and never let it go. It's the basis of all history. It's why the world was created. It tells the purpose of life, and opens up the future. It's the reason for the cross and for salvation. And it explains why the divine Word became flesh in the man Jesus. In the beginning, when God created the heavens and the earth, he was both matter and spirit, together. Matter and Spirit were One.

But then something wondrous and amazing happened. God had been contemplating metamorphosis for himself. He had been wanting a change. So, he decided that he would temporarily separate his Body from his Spirit, transform it, and return it to himself renewed and revitalized. He would form for himself a new body to serve him and do his desire, an Eve to share with him the unbounded, uncharted future. So God spoke the word of his wishes, and separated the visible out from the invisible. He formed our world; earth, air, and water. The divine Body and Spirit were torn temporarily apart. Matter and Spirit were differentiated.

This idea, that God's Body and Spirit were split apart by the act of creation, is novel of course. It can sound brash and impudent to ears attuned to the oft-repeated refrain that God is pure, disembodied Spirit. For most Christians, God is a ghost. To put a face on this holy ghost may seem inordinate and immodest. But to put him in a body? A Body?

It grows even more shocking when we realize that separation of a spirit from its body is death!

Incredibly, the creation of the world involved the death of God! Yes, child, God died! Unbelievably, death was central to God's plan from the beginning, and it included God himself first of all. As the great archetype and pattern, the Creator died so that the world might live. The act of creation was the death of God. He died for his bride. There is no greater love. As the archetypal pattern, God died for the world.

But death could not destroy him, of course. Death cannot destroy the Eternal One. He's indestructible. Looking back from the cross, we can see that his death was meant to be temporary, just an interlude, an interregnum, three divinely planned and appointed periods of separation between the divine Body and Spirit. The Spirit would remain apart from the world for three eras or dispensations, for three "days."

The cross re-defined death for all time. Calvary's lesson is that death for Christ and for those joined to him is just a temporary disengagement between body and spirit. Jesus' death was just a three-day journey of separation. And because he is the exact image of God, his death imaged the primordial act of creation. The cross was a look backward and upward. Jesus' resurrection showed clearly and convincingly that death does not always mean destruction. It can be a positive thing. In the shadow of the cross, the death of God is not such a wild and outlandish idea. The resurrection of Jesus brought a new understanding of death. It brought hope into the world, and shined a new light on the creation. And astonishingly, it was a revelation of God.

This truth, like the others, has always been there, right in the center of the Gospel story, nailed to the cross for all to see, but covered over by the heavy shroud of accumulated tradition. Yet the very heart of the Gospel is the bedrock truth that Christ Jesus was the true image and revelation of God. The truth of Calvary is that death, for God and for humans in whom God lives, is not destruction.

And, like Father like Sons. For all of God's children, with whom the Spirit has united, who are themselves made in the image of God, death is just a temporary disconnect. The saints too, like Christ Jesus, are images of God. Their death is like his. The lesson of the cross is that the death of the saints is not destruction, but rather just a temporary separation between body and spirit. The death of his children echoes the death of their heavenly Father. They image him. Every saint's story becomes the abridged and oft-repeated story of God, with the same plot and outcome as that of their Creator and Savior. It's a story well worth knowing, and worth repeating to everyone.

Like him, the saints too are holy. And true holiness is separation from this world. Death in Christ sanctifies the saints. But they're not destroyed. Nor are they left forever bodiless. Death, as with their Savior and as with their Creator whom they image, has no power over them. Death with Christ is their physical as well as spiritual sanctification, not their destruction. It's what makes them saints, that is, holy ones. But like their Savior, it does not make them mere holy ghosts. They become part of the body of Christ, which is made of matter and spirit. And Christ is God. The body of Christ is the body of God. God has—or rather is—a Body as well as a Spirit. And it's growing. Golgotha's tomb is empty.

We can be assured, then, that the act of creation, which was the death of God, was his sanctification, not his destruction. It was his separation from the world. God himself is the first Saint! Holy, holy, holy is the Lord Almighty, Creator of heaven and earth. Yes, child, rest assured that death for the Creator and for his children is their sanctification, not their destruction. The saints' separation from this world gives them a place in the new creation that is presently being formed. This was the divine plan from the beginning. Matter and Spirit have never been incompatible or irreconcilable. Their present differentiation is just temporary.

The new creation in fact involves the reconciliation of body and spirit. They will be reunited into oneness. And when the divine Spirit and Body come together again as One in the Resurrection, the saints will not be just spectators cheering from the bleachers. They themselves will be participants in this gala celestial reunion. They will be lovingly gathered back into the divine Oneness that existed before the creation of the world (John 17:5, 21-23). Yes, child, believe it. The saints will be lovingly gathered in to the divine Oneness, immersed into the very sacrosanct Spirit and Body of God (2 Peter 1:4)!

Meanwhile, history marches steadily and unswervingly toward this incredible climax. We can see this when we become friends with the biblical record. We must take it down from the shelf, dust it off, open it, and listen carefully to what it says. We must read it free of the shroud of orthodoxy and tradition, face to face, eyeball to eyeball. Like Jacob, we must go *mano a mano* with it, all night if need be. The Bible reveals the overarching plot of history, from beginning to end, from sunrise to sundown and beyond, but only to its friends. It tells its secrets only to those willing to come to grips with the truth, wherever it leads, even if the truth contradicts tradition and upsets the status quo.

It tells us that one day not so far past, about 2,000 years ago, an exemplary human was born in whom Creator and creation would come together again. In the man Jesus, Spirit and Body were reunited (Matt. 3:16-17; John 1:14). At his baptism, Jesus began the reunion of heaven and earth, becoming the firstborn of the new creation. The long-awaited reconciliation began beside the Jordan, and continued on through Jesus' death and resurrection to glory. With Jesus' baptism, God has begun reconstituting his Body.

Because of Jesus' oneness with the Spirit, death could not destroy him. It was just a brief interlude imaging God, three short days of separation between Body and Spirit. The divine death pattern was repeated. Then he was resurrected, again echoing the archetypal pattern. In Christ Jesus, the divine Spirit and Body, separated in the creation, began the long-awaited process of coming together again in glorious and loving reunion.

In Jesus, the Resurrection of God has begun!

The cross event, at the center of all human history, was a re-enactment of the creation story. Calvary was a creation event, the start of a new world, and repeats the divine archetype, for Jesus is the true image of God (2 Cor. 4:4; Col. 1:15). The Jesus story is God's story, condensed and translated into human terms. And he is the firstfruits. The harvest of saints that follows will be like him. They too, repeat the divine archetype. They too will participate in the Resurrection of God.

Yes, the archetype of death and resurrection that resonated around the cross is a recurrent motif that sounded right from the very beginning, and it rings throughout the whole record of God's dealings with humankind. It's a song about dying and rising again unto greater glories. Its soothing lyrics bring comfort to the dying saints, reassuring us that death with Christ is not destruction, nor is it to be feared. It sings softly that death for the saints is actually a new birth, a time of renewal and a time for rejoicing. For every saint, to live is Christ and to die is gain. Death for the saints has become a doorway into life, abundant and free, and unimaginably glorious. The Gospel is a lullaby to sing God's little ones to sleep.

The true Gospel is a cradlesong about life arising from death. It sings through the lives of the saints as it did through the life of Jesus. Not surprisingly, their lives repeat the same lyrical harmonies, for they too have a cross to carry. And like Jesus, they are being changed from glory to glory, into the likeness of Christ, through their own death and resurrection.

That's the truth the Bible tells its friends. The archetype is at its very center, so we won't miss it. It's a revelation and re-enactment of God's plans and purposes for himself and for the world. It's God's self-portrait, his confession, a song of life ever victorious over death, of existence ever triumphant over nonexistence. And believers are invited to join with the Creator in singing the same story with their lips and with their lives.

God wants us to see that the vast panorama of history displays this same pattern. As we open our Bible carefully, and remove the shroud of false tradition from off its pages, we can enter into its story and climb its highest mountain. From there, the whole horizon of human history, west to east, will open before us. Gazing then at sunrise and sunset of world history, at creation's morning and evening, we'll realize that the Word of God is standing here with us, at the center of this spreading vista. What's going on? What's happening, and what does it mean?

God's Desire for Change

God is changing. To speak is to change. In the beginning, God spoke our world into being, and God was changed. Even before the creation, the divine Word was active, deep in the heart of God, communing with him, sharing in the divine self-awareness. The Word was with God and the Word was God (John 1:1-3). And as he spoke, he changed.

And God has not become mute. He still speaks. He's here with us today, still speaking and still changing. His Word keeps company with us just as he once kept company with God. When we are made into his image and likeness, the Word speaks within our hearts just as he once spoke within the heart of God. Yes, amazingly, the very Creator himself is right here with us, and lives in us, and talks to us if we'll listen. And his Word still produces change. It's still creative.

The Word of God is not just a series of sounds, or scribblings on old manuscripts or pieces of paper. It's alive, and powerful. As it is spoken, it forms reality. It causes things to come forward, dressing them with substance, time, and place. And wonderfully, the Word is creative in the mouth of the saints as it was in the beginning with God. It has not lost its power. The Word is an expression of the divine, whether spoken by God or by men in and through whom God speaks. Herein is the miraculous power in the Gospel, and in the prayer of faith that finds its answer every time.

It's why we were given the gift of language, the capacity for speech. It was to ready us for the Word! He intended that humans too, like himself, would have the Word in their hearts, and on their lips, with all its awesome, miracle-making power. He's preparing us. He's readying us for our future.

In the beginning, God had plans, big plans. He would reproduce himself. He would engender a Son in his likeness. In fact, he would have many children, numerous as the stars of heaven, abundant as the sand of the seashore. And being his children they would bear his image. He would provide clues by which they could find him. While he was creating he would employ archetypes and foreshadowings, hints of himself and his purposes so that they could sense his presence and seek him. It would be a treasure hunt, and he himself would be the incalculable goal and reward of their searching (Acts 17:26-27).

Some of these archetypes would be written down carefully, so that when the time was fully come, the dull of hearing could hear, and the blind could see. They would see, and believe, and trustingly come to him. His message of victory over death, spoken from the beginning and written in his word, would take hold in their hearts and come alive in them. They would receive him, and the Spirit and the creation would be reunited in loving communion and fellowship. Yes, they would come to him, one believer at a time. Then, after three days, Spirit and Body would be reconstituted. Earth and heaven would be reconciled.

Indeed, the first creation itself, this present world, is an archetype, the handiwork of God's Word. It foreshadows the new creation, which began at Jesus' baptism and hurried on to Calvary, where a bright new world began to form from the death of the divine once more. The cross event was a creation event, the start of a new creation. And it repeats the archetype. It mirrors the first creation. The cross envisions the entire sweep of history, from start to finish. This present world itself will undergo the change that God envisioned for himself. The creation has a cross to bear.

Looking back from Calvary, we can see that the death of God in the first creation was the temporary separation of the Body from the Spirit. But also, as at the cross, death could not destroy him. It merely changed him, from glory to glory. Matter and Spirit were differentiated, but not forever. Through his death and resurrection, God would make for himself a new, transformed Body, a living Temple. This world will become the new Temple of the Spirit. It's happening right now, all around us. We're smack in the middle of divine history, people. We're part of the epic, all-encompassing story of God. Can you see the wonder of it? Can you feel the excitement? Are you playing your part well?

Transformation and new life through death is the Gospel's central theme. It's the bedrock purpose for the creation and for human existence. For the saints as for Christ, death is just a temporary separation, a change of body to be consummated at the Resurrection. And this change, the very soul of the Bible, images and includes the Creator himself! God is changing. He is metamorphosing. That was his plan since even before the creation. Change in God and in the creation comes from the expression of God's creative Word, as God's will is expressed.

As he reflected, before ever the world was, pondering divine things too deep for human understanding, the Creator determined on a special objective. He would change his manner of existence. Yes, he would express his heart's desire and create a Bride for himself, a helpmeet with whom to share his dreams and his future. And so he spoke the Word, and it flew out instantly from the heart of God, bursting from his lips into the boundless expanses. It formed itself into our world.

This purpose bears repeating. God's nature is expressed in creating. He's the Creator. His nature is to create, to induce change. It's what he does. In the infinite stretches of time, deep in the veiled mists of eternity before this world took form, God desired a change in his manner of being. So, in ways beyond human comprehension or language, he expressed himself, and our world came to be. The reality that we know today had a godly beginning. The beginning of our world was the differentiation between the divine Matter and Spirit.

The Bible says that he spoke and, voilá, it happened! Our world of today was born from the expression of the Creator, wrapped in the swaddling bands of the divine purpose, crying out the first baby cries of his will (Rom. 11:36). Our world is God's strong, emphatic statement that he is changing. To create is to change. Change is the main sentence in the paragraph of this world. It's the subject and the predicate of every sentence that he speaks. As he speaks, God is metamorphosing. His full metamorphosis will be realized in the fullness of Christ. Christ is the complete Word of God, a complete sentence. More than that, he is an epic novel, the Creator's full expression, Alpha to Omega.

God is immensely articulate. Early in creation's morning his Word rang out, echoing down the long, endless halls of time and space. We can still hear it resonating in the cycles of nature, pulsing with life and energy, pounding as though the world had a heart. The creation sings and sways to a rhythm far greater than human lifetimes. The song is the Creator's dynamic assertion of himself, alive and vastly powerful, able to fulfill itself unfailingly in perfect realization of his will (1 Cor. 8:6; 2 Cor. 5:18).

The Word of God, being the expression of the Creator, creates. It forms reality. It clothes possibilities with substance, time, and place, and fulfills itself by determining its own truth. It's a self-fulfilling prophecy. God's Word formed the world, and keeps it moving on its predetermined course (Heb. 1:1-3; Col. 1:17). His Word reaches out and draws new realities from the unfathomable ocean of his will, pulling the nonexistent into existence, making the dreams of God come true (Rom. 4:17). The Word is alive, and pulses with creative power.

The Word of Creation

God's Word does not depend, then, on the world. Rather, the world is dependent on God's Word. The Word is first, and the world follows. It's Word before world. The Word says what will be, and it becomes (John 1:3). Spirit commands matter like a sergeant commands a private. Matter serves the whims of the Spirit. It's mind over matter. God's Word of truth tells the future to come forth, and it does. His Word is the power in prophecy that never fails, and the dynamism in the prayer of faith.

His Word is the activating force that creates reality and upholds it (Heb. 1:3). It works in accordance with God's will. The Word flies ahead of the world and pulls it forward with the strong, inescapable tractor beam of God's purpose (Heb. 11:3; 2 Peter 3:5-7). The divine assertion is sovereign and supreme, self-empowered, infinitely potent and energized.

The Bible says that, in the beginning, God spoke his will into being (Ps. 33:9). His Word took hold in the infinite stretches of time and space and formed the world that we see all around us, pregnant with divine promise, teeming with possibilities. As it began its pre-planned journey, always under the watchful care of its Creator, the world was pleasing to its supremely eloquent Speaker. It had turned out well, just as he had wanted. It was good. His Word was well spoken.

Was there a Big Bang, as many scientists believe? If so, it was because of the Big Word. In any event, this world in which we live had a beginning. It hasn't always existed. It had a start. Scientists trace the beginning of the universe as we know it to a point in time and space, but cannot go further back. They can only guess at what was there before the Big Bang. They don't know what's beyond the bang of creation.

The Bible goes further, and tells us of the self-existent One who dwells in eternity. He was there in the beginning, speaking the Word of his good pleasure, delightedly watching it accomplish his anticipated goals. And he is present today, still watching the world develop according to his will. And he will be here tomorrow, satisfied in the fulfillment of his dreams.

But the Bible is not concerned with the creation of the cosmos. Its focus is narrower. Its gaze is upon our world, and especially on the humans who inhabit it. The creation account is about the world of today, the world of clouds and oceans and peoples. It's not concerned with the start of the measureless universe. The Bible is like an ever burning bush that grabs our attention and draws us to God and holiness. This world becomes holy ground in its light. Holiness is the purpose of human life, and the reason for our world, where flowers bloom and robins fly, and humans learn to speak. And a few fortunate ones repeat the divine story with their words and with their lives.

God's Desire to Merge

When the Bible speaks of God's Word, or when it portrays God speaking, that's an anthropomorphism. It speaks of God as if he were human, as we are doing here. Our method is entirely harmonious with the biblical pattern. In the Bible God speaks, and laughs and shouts. He becomes angry or jealous, rides on the wings of the wind, and so forth. These are metaphors, figurative ways to envision God. They help us to understand his intents and purposes, and our relationship with him. They place him within our realm of experience. We can relate to him, as if he were one of us. The anthropomorphisms in the Bible help us to understand God in human terms. They bring him down to earth. And if you listen carefully you can hear in them a faint, barely audible whisper of the incarnation of Christ.

One vitally important thing they tell us is that God is in some sense a Speaker. He expresses himself. And, since the world is the result of God's expression, it reveals him. It has purpose and direction. Learning about the world is like listening to what God has said about himself. To help us better understand the world, and his will, he has graciously given us the Bible. Anthropomorphisms in the Bible are like written musical notes in a song written by the Master Composer. Notably, they sing of God as if he were one of us! We must listen closely to the song, so that we can learn to step to the rhythm of God's purposes. We'll want to dance and sing in harmony with the Spirit. Imagine the honor. With his word, God invites us to be his dancing partner!

His word is an invitation, and in it he uses types and figures, pictures and metaphors. They are more than just literary devices or figures of speech. They are clues, pieces of a giant mosaic that paints the whole of history, from beginning to end and on past. They work together to form a picture of the Creator and his plans, and the reason of our creation. The anthropomorphisms in the Bible actually point forward to a marvelous and incredible truth about God to be fully revealed when his purposes are finalized. We should listen carefully as they speak of God in human terms. There are lessons for us in the archetypes and patterns.

God purposely presents himself in the Bible as a Being with human attributes and characteristics like us, because his intention is actually to merge with humanity. He wants us to be like him. He desires real fellowship. Incredibly, he is merging humanity into the divine glory!

This astounding truth is the epic story that the Bible tells. It's the big picture, the main theme not only of the Bible, but of the whole creation. The stupendous, cosmic truth that the Scriptures reveal and that Jesus demonstrates is that the exalted and majestic One who created the world is taking human nature to himself, embodied, to share his divine life and glory with us! The Creator has chosen to receive us into himself. Yes, dear one, in the all-consuming reconciliation of the world, the saints will be merged into God and become One with the Creator!

This is the plan of the ages, the grand design that the Word and the world express, speaking the will and purposes of God into reality, telling of his glories (Ps. 19:1-3). Humanity is in the center of God's purpose. He desires that you and I and all our friends understand his will and receive his Spirit. His plan is to reconcile the world to himself, literally. And he wants our company. We are called to give our lives fully to the divine will. Those who do so will be transformed and readied for this astounding destiny of re-assimilation into the divine inner life of the Creator. Yes, child, the glory that God has promised isn't just whistling Dixie. His plans are absolutely breathtaking, far beyond our wildest imaginations.

Metaphorical, but Real

So, when the Bible portrays God speaking, as if it were a human trait or characteristic, we should take it in a natural sense, realizing that it is metaphorical, and try to understand the truth he wants to convey. God speaks in various ways. He talks to us in the words and events of the Scriptures, but also in the ebb and flow of existence. His voice can be heard in the steady march of the seasons, and in the fields of grain and in the lush hillsides. He's present in the rain that falls, and in the lowing of cattle. He communicates to us in the fulfillment of prophecies, in our daily lives, and in the currents of history.

The creation is God's handiwork. It speaks, in the language of heaven, and proudly tells of his glories to whoever will listen (Ps. 19:1-6). It smiles and whispers of indescribable wonders and unimaginable splendors. The Bible is a tour guide that points out the presence of God in the world all around us. The prime showpiece is the Son, the Word who took human form in order to accomplish the purposes of God.

The incarnation of the Word in Christ Jesus is the central message of the Bible. He is its most aromatic flower, its sweetest fragrance. To read the Bible with understanding is like taking a walk through an arboretum filled with beautiful, scented flowers and exotic plants. Each new sight and smell reveals Christ in a new way, and fills us with fresh wonder and delight. Every new turn reveals more exquisite displays, richer discoveries and greater joys.

As we become friends with his word, we come upon ever fresh and exciting glimpses of our Maker. With each new insight he becomes ever more glorious. It makes us eager for more truth. His word is at once satisfying and intriguing. It lifts us up out of the choking smog and pollution of this world into the open expanses of heaven. God's word reveals the Creator's plans, his blueprints for the dazzling project he is preparing for eternity. It reveals Christ. God's word is his revealing. He wants us to understand it.

Faith and the Laws of Physics

But we are not yet capable of understanding in the way that God understands. We do not yet understand the flow of reality, how the nonexistent future becomes instantly real in the present, and then just as mysteriously runs on past us and disappears. We ourselves are caught in the undertow of time and place. The persons we were yesterday are gone. Where did we go? The world still contains inexplicable mysteries. We do not know how God's Word works. We do not yet know in the way that we are known (1 Cor. 13:12).

We do not understand creation. As yet, we cannot tell the process by which Body and Spirit were differentiated into their distinct qualities and characteristics, nor how they still continue to interact. They were pulled apart and differentiated, but nevertheless they remain in contact, for although God and the world are separated, the Spirit continues to move within the world, and in our hearts. The Spirit is everywhere, as is the Word, but we don't know how. We don't know how matter and spirit interact.

But we do know that everything in this material world owes its existence to something beyond itself, something prior. All things have originated through a process of development. Nothing here can be its own cause, or generate itself from nonexistence. The constant flow of the creation thus points to the Creator. Because it is created, the world in its present state is not eternal. It originated from God as he expressed himself. The Bible tells us that this world came from God and will return to him (Rom. 11:36; 1 Cor. 8:6, 11:12).

God is the ultimate source, substance, and goal of all things, and the one who ultimately determines how and why things are. As we learn more about the laws that operate in the world, we learn more about how God's Word works. And he reassures us that he has a purpose that includes us. That's what matters. Yes, that's what matters!

Our world did not originate from itself, then. It came from God (Rom. 11:36; 1 Cor. 11:12). History doesn't run blind. It is following the course on which God sent it. Our world was not created to remain static. It is unfailingly accomplishing the work assigned to it. Nor was it formed in an instantaneous creation. God has plenty of time, and patience.

In creating this world, he placed in it internal processes, what we call natural laws, to temporarily separate it from him and carry it away toward a predetermined stopping point. The world had a beginning, and it will have an end. It will be returned to its Maker by an even greater power than separation. Meanwhile, those original and originating laws and processes of separation are still active. The Bible calls them principalities and powers. They ever strive to pull the world away from God, following their assigned function. The creation still struggles to separate itself from its Creator, obeying its original prime directive, accomplishing God's holiness.

These physical laws and principles by which humans try to explain this natural world are God's handiwork. He placed them here and gave them their orders. But no one really understands what they are, or how they operate, or why. Humans do not know, for example, what energy or magnetism really are. These are just names for something beyond us, whose effects we see. We call them natural laws, and imagine them with or without a Lawgiver. Our understanding is limited. Is energy real? Yes, it is, for we can see its influence. But we don't really understand it, or how it works or why. We just know that it's there, and it seems to be regular. Has anyone ever seen it? No, but we know it exists and we rely on it because we see and feel its effects. We experience its workings. We know it's there because we can discover regularities that seem to occur repeatedly. We call these regularities laws.

That's how we accept God's Word. It's like energy, unseen but real, and always ready to work (John 3:8). God's Word is the very energy of creation. But faith does not consist of blind loyalty. We believe in the truth of God's word because we have seen its influence and tested its results. We know it is real and potent because we have experienced its power and understood its logic. It has spoken through the prophets, and it told the truth, beforehand. The prophecies have come true, the promises have all been faithful. Not one of them has proved untrue.

The archetypes and foreshadowings in the Bible are strong, irrefutable evidence of God's truth. We have seen his Word become real in the world, and felt its pull. It has carried us to the mountaintops. From there, as we look out in wonder upon the stretching vistas and widening expanses, we understand more and more its logic and truth, and its sheer magnitude. We can't help but feel awed and amazed. And our faith grows, based on truth.

True faith holds hands with understanding. The more we understand God's truths, the more we can step in harmony with his will. Trust in God's Word deepens as we understand the message, verify its truth, and find it perfectly reasonable and real. Through his word, we hear the honeyed voice of God, and feel his warm caress. We can hear God's voice singing his beneficent presence, plans, and influence all around us. And we can feel his comforting Spirit in our hearts, speaking soft and gentle love-words to us. We must listen as he sings of resplendent ages gone by, and of others even more resplendent just beyond the sun-blazed horizon.

Those things that once appeared fearful and unnerving, he turns into blessings and joys. Even death itself has been wrestled to the ground. Its terrors no longer hold us. His word sings a lullaby of God's presence with us to lighten the darkness and chase away the horrors hiding there. The terrors of night must not frighten us. We must listen to God's soothing voice. We must peruse the pages of his word, and ponder its pictures.

Freedom and Other Wild Horses

As we read, we can see a wildness within the world (Gen. 1:28). The natural laws that God purposely placed in the creation to rule here, the principalities and powers, were born with an instinct to freedom. They keep the world skittish, always running from him, like a herd of wild horses. And this wildness runs amok in the human heart. Immersed fully in the creation, we too run from God. But he likes horses with spirit. They are never beyond his control. He doesn't fear to give humans freedom to roam in his pasture.

Freedom, like the other laws, is not a Frankenstein. The human heart is not too wild and fierce for God. The liberty he gives us to develop and grow, and to choose him or reject him, cannot break the Creator's fence. He throws the bridle of his Word over the world, and makes it carry him where he wishes. He is the Creator. All things accomplish his will. Even the wild horses of unbelief and self-service he makes to serve him and in their service glorify him.

None of the principalities or powers he placed in the world and in our heart circumvents or destroys the Creator's designs. They serve him. Ultimately, the whole world will be lassoed and brought back to God in Christ. He is God's Word and his will, the reins in the Creator's hands (Col. 1:17; Heb. 1:3). The world, wild as it is, is bridled and controlled by the Word of God. It will fulfill his purpose of metamorphosis. His Body will be reconstituted.

God's Real Presence in the Creation

When God expressed the world into existence, he smiled and told of its end as well. The same dynamic, empowered, and unstoppable Word that began this world will talk it through to its indescribably glorious destiny. As surely as this world exists, just as surely will God's faithful and fulfilling Word return to him having accomplished the predetermined purposes of its divine Speaker. The Gospel is the Word of reconciliation (Ps. 55:10-11).

The drama is already written, with an all-star cast and an ending that's out of this world. Soon the accomplished Word of God will emerge from behind the dark curtain of the future and will walk into the light of center stage. The entire company will be gathered. Dancers, singers, musicians, all will come together for the final extravaganza. And earth's last scene will be a grand finale of cosmic grandeur, for God is its Director. Meanwhile, tickets are still available.

God Is in Everything

The events and processes that form our world have always performed under God's watchful eye, giving him great satisfaction. He is busy all over the set, and in the audience. His unseen presence touches everything in the creation, giving it direction, energizing it, and enabling it to play its role. The divine Director holds the curtain of the future, and runs the lights. His Word is everywhere, building the set, coaching the actors, helping them learn their lines, giving them their cues. He greatly desires the performance to be a good one. God's presence within the world works to assure its success. The Grand Finale must be an event to be remembered for all time.

He was there in the beginning when the first curtain went up. The Holy Spirit was present and active as God spoke the creating Word at the start. The world took its present form as the Spirit moved upon the face of the waters (Gen. 1:2). He's still present, working behind the scenes. The world hasn't been left totally alone. The Spirit is still active everywhere, unseen, guiding the world to its predetermined future, doing everything necessary to ensure that the performance is perfect from beginning to end.

The Spirit knows firsthand the mind of God (1 Cor. 2:11). He closely oversees the world's progress, moving on ahead, clearing the way before it, helping it across. God's involvement in the world nudges history freely in the direction that he wishes. He guides it by his presence. His Spirit inheres within the divine Word (John 6:63; 2 Tim. 2:16). The Word of God is God.

Mary Says Yes

And so, with the passage of time, in the natural course of events guided by the Holy Spirit according to the Word of God, one tiny part of this world became a Jewish virgin named Mary. And she was formed with freedom of choice.

God didn't fear her free choice. Nor did Mary fear giving herself to the working of God's will. The wild steed of freedom was strangely tame and gentle in the heart of this Jewish maiden. Mary's reception of the word spoken by the angel was her acquiescence and commitment to the great eternal purposes of God. Her free choice brought her personally into harmony with the divine heartbeat. It made her an active participant in God's plan of the ages. Her acquiescence gave her a share in the story and glory of God.

At the proper time, an angel was sent to maiden Mary to communicate to her the divine will. Upon receiving this word from heaven she acquiesced, and trustingly placed herself within the superbly grand designs and purposes of God. The Spirit overshadowed her, and she conceived a boy child. And they named him Jesus, in obedience to God's word spoken to her by the angel (Luke 1:35, 2:21). The Word of God was powerfully present in these events.

Mary's decision to receive the Spirit was an example and a foreshadowing. In faith she freely chose to believe God's word and accept his will, inviting the Holy Spirit to overshadow her. She placed her life into harmony with the creative Word spoken from the beginning. She was stepping in tempo with the strong, steady beat of God's own heart.

The conception of Jesus was through the natural laws and processes spoken from the beginning. It was a natural birth. When the child took on flesh in virgin womb, it was according to the working of the same creative and prophetic Word that was with God in the beginning. All things of this world have come by the same powerful and dynamic Word (John 1:1-3; 1 Cor. 8:6; Heb. 1:2). His birth was according to the same natural laws by which all babies are born, except for one thing. Mary was a virgin. Her child was a special one.

Now, after the patient, careful passage of eons, with everything in place and with perfect timing, the word of creation was fulfilled in a unique and very special way. Natural processes spoken into place from the beginning were voiced anew now to Mary, and were accomplished in her with absolute precision. The prophecies were fulfilled, flawlessly.

A Natural Birth

This was not the first time the Word of God caused a baby to be born, or the only time, or the last. This same incarnation happens in every human, indeed in every beast of the earth and bird of the sky, and in every fish of the sea (John 1:1-3). But this time it was special. This time the Word paused, cleared his throat, and concentrated on what he was to say. He must not stutter, nor mispronounce any of the words. He would express clearly this special embodiment about to occur.

Jesus was the cornerstone for God's entire project. On him would rest its success or failure. The Spirit drew his breath and spoke, clearly and emphatically. The word rang out with vibrancy and power. It would echo down the long corridors of eternity. Here was God's promise to the world. God had given his word in these events. The universe turned with bated breath and waited and watched, wondering, listening expectantly. In the silent night there sounded the still, small cries of a human baby! And the angels glorified God in the highest.

The Fruit of Mary's Womb

This Son of David, child of Mary, was born through the direct involvement of God, who caused Mary to conceive while she remained yet a virgin. Mary became pregnant miraculously through the empowering, orchestrating presence and direction of the Spirit. In the Babe of Bethlehem, the Spirit-infused Word spoken from the beginning was being fulfilled. But as we shall see, it was not as the churches have explained it.

God did not violate Mary's virginity, or impregnate her. That would have been adultery. And Jesus would have been illegitimate. Rather, God empowered Mary to conceive from her own body. Jesus was not a spirit being who entered Mary's womb. His birth wasn't the result of a womb invasion. All created things come into existence through the same Word who was with God and who was God in the beginning (John 1:1-3). Although the conception of Jesus was unique and miraculous, it was natural. He shared in the same createdness and processes of nature that were put in place from the start. He was born human.

It was a new, unique and extraordinary event, the first and only time ever of a virgin becoming pregnant and giving birth. But it involved processes spoken into the world from the beginning. In the natural course of time, in keeping with God's plan, the creation had now become pregnant with the human who would one day be called God's firstborn Son. Mary had become pregnant with Jesus. As yet, however, contrary to tradition, his divine sonship was still only figurative. It awaited his baptism in the Spirit. Jesus' birth was unique, but natural. It was not God, or one-third of him, who was born in Bethlehem. It was Jesus, fully human and only human, miraculously yes, but nevertheless only human.

Jesus would be called the Son of God, the angel said, because the Spirit would overshadow Mary and empower her to conceive (Luke 1:35). But God didn't impregnate her. Jesus was fully a part of the creation. Created things always derive from something prior, always, without exception. That's what God's word says. And Jesus was a real, bona fide human. That's what God's word says as well. The Son of Man, being fully human and earth-made, was given form by the body of Mary his mother. He was the fruit of her womb (Luke 1:42). He grew to manhood by assimilating to himself the food, air, and water of Galilee. He shared fully in earthly life. Like the rest of us, he was a child of the planet earth, its loveliest and best.

The Rebirth of Jesus

But he was also called the Son of God. What does that mean? Here we must give a powerful yank at the shroud of tradition. It's heavy, and resists being removed. But when the baby Jesus is foretold to be the Son of God it doesn't mean that God had any sort of sexual relations with Mary. Nor does it mean that Jesus was born God the Son. He was son of Mary, seed of David. God was yet his Father only figuratively. The Spirit had enabled her to conceive parthenogenically, virginally, without male partner.

Upon being told that she would conceive, Mary inquired, "How shall this be, since I know not a man (Luke 1:34)?" The angelic response was that the Spirit would come upon her, and the power of the Most High would overshadow (invest, enable) her. But God would not impregnate her with himself, an act that would have constituted adultery and that would have made the child illegitimate. Jesus was not illegitimate, a child of fornication as the tradition of a spiritual impregnation would imply.

Yes, Jesus would be called the Son of God, but he was not alone. Every Israelite was God's firstborn (Exod. 4:22; Hos. 11:1; Luke 1:34-35, 11:13, etc.). Every Jewish male baby was called a son of God. But it was merely metaphorical. God was the Father of Israel not because he impregnated every Jewish mother with himself, or materialized in her womb, but rather because he had in ancient times orchestrated the events surrounding the figurative "birth" of Israel. His fatherhood of Israel was the result of his orchestration of the events surrounding their figurative birth, and his protection for their growth. At birth the baby Jesus was a son of God in the same way that every male Jew was a son of God. His true divine sonship would come thirty years later.

The Spirit's overshadowing of the maiden Mary was an empowerment. God was not her sexual partner. The Spirit empowered her temporarily in the manner that Old Testament prophets were empowered. His birth was still in the time of Law. It was miraculous but not, excuse me, an act of rape or consensual fornication. God did not violate her. It was an empowerment of Mary, not an engendering by God.

It should go without saying, obviously, that Jesus did not exist before he was conceived. The Word and the Spirit existed from the beginning, but the human Jesus came into being in Mary's womb. When he says he descended from heaven, that he existed before Abraham, at that point he is no longer merely human (John 1:30, 3:13, 31, 6:33, 62, 8:42, 58, 17:5; Phil. 2:6; Col. 1:16-17, etc.). He is by then reunited with God in shared identity, having received the Spirit at his baptism. He is speaking of his new nature after his baptism in the Spirit. He is now One with God. God became his true Father at the Jordan (Matt. 3:17). Jesus' divine sonship was the direct result of his Spirit baptism. Jesus was born again!

At the start of his ministry he emphasized that humans cannot enter the kingdom of God unless they are begotten of water and wind, that is, of the Spirit (John 3:5). He was not an exception, nor did he ever claim to be. Like his brethren, he too underwent baptism in the Spirit as well as in water (Luke 3:22). Flesh and blood, ordinary humanity, cannot inherit the kingdom of heaven (1 Cor. 15:50). To enter, humans must be reunited with God. Flesh must reunite with Spirit. And that happens by reception of the Spirit. It comes by receiving Christ.

It's true that Jesus claimed that he was not of this world. But he said the same thing about his true followers. God's other children are not of this world in the same manner in which Jesus is not of this world (John 15:18-19, 17:16-18; 1 John 4:4-6). We, too, saints every one and God's other children, are from God too, sent into the world in the same way that Jesus was sent. He is our leader, guide, and older brother. In him, humanity was joined with divinity as the firstfruits, the precursor of many who would follow (Rom. 8:9, 11). We, too, are not of this world, child, if we have been born of the Spirit, reconciled with God and made One with our Savior. Like Jesus, we and the Father are One. We are the inheritors of heaven. Don't be afraid to claim your inheritance. And don't let anyone steal it from you. It's your God-given gift. We are co-inheritors with Christ (Rom. 8:17).

Jesus was made like us in all things (Heb. 2:17). If that's true, then we are like him in all things. And it is true. Like him, Jesus' brethren are begotten of God when they receive his Spirit (John 1:13). God's Spirit-infused Word becomes flesh anew whenever a person receives the Spirit of Christ. It's a joining together, but it's not through sexual relations (John 1:12-13). Nor is it a materializing. The Creator at that point becomes our true spiritual Father (John 20:17; Heb. 2:11). Our spiritual mother is Zion (Gal. 4:26). Like us, Jesus became the true Son of God not at his conception, but at his baptism. Until then, it was his destiny, his certain and secure future. He would become the true Son of God when he received baptism in the Spirit.

The Spirit came upon Mary in the same way that he came upon others in the Old Testament (Luke 1:15, 41, 67, 2:25). Her pregnancy was before Pentecost, in the time of Law, a temporary empowerment, and prefigurative, in accordance with the purpose of the Old Testament (Gal. 3:24). At birth Jesus' divine Sonship, kingship, priesthood, and Lordship were in their eminent perfection still future (Phil. 2:8-11; Heb 1:4, 2:10). Jesus became the Christ, the Anointed one, when he was anointed. It happened when he received the seal of the Spirit. He was exalted through the Spirit to the throne of glory only after his death. Mary was not the mother of God. She was the mother of Jesus. Like you and I, Jesus was a product of the earth.

A Living Planet

Even though the Spirit and the Body were separated in the beginning, God's Spirit and Word have never completely left the world in absolute isolation. His divine, living, and inspired Word has in fact formed the world (Acts 17:28; Heb. 1:1-3). The world is the result of the expression of God. It's the instantiation of his spoken, creative Word. The divine Word is alive and dynamic, indwelt by the Spirit and swarming with all the power of heaven itself. The Word of God is alive (Heb. 4:12).

The world, being the expression of the Word, is alive too! In Genesis we read that God commanded the earth to bring forth. And with the divine command came the power to comply. The Word enabled the earth to bring forth life from itself. Life did not invade our planet. Life has been inherent within it even from the start (1 Tim. 6:13). The miracle of growth originates within the earth itself. As humans, animals, and plants grow, their bodies take on more and more of the living earth. This added growth is fully alive too, bursting with vitality and energy. The tree is as fully alive as the acorn. The cat is as fully alive as the kitten. The wee life in the child is still there, but larger, in the adult. From where has this added life come?

It has come from the earth. The boy has grown into a man by assimilating the earth to himself, slowly, in careful, measured mouthfuls. In his eating, he has added life to himself from the living earth. He has grown from the ground on which bountifully grow the corn and the wheat. He has drunk daily from the showers that have watered the rich, fertile loam of which he is made. And he has put forth his hand and eaten of the trees of the garden. The earth has given him life because the earth itself is alive.

Springtime will lead into summer, then autumn, and the cold days of winter. And the boy will return to whence he came. He will relinquish his life to the same living earth from which he emerged, ashes to ashes and dust to dust (Gen. 3:19). The same earth that once proudly gave him life will stretch out her arms and draw him back into her bosom. In his place she will nourish some other boy, who will eat the corn and the wheat that grow in the rich, fertile soil that once was vibrant with laughter and all the dreams of boyhood. And this other boy will grow tall and strong, and flourish for a while. The cycle will be repeated.

Yes, our planet is alive (1 Tim. 6:13). At God's command the earth gave birth to the living. Life is inherent in the clay (Acts 7:38; Heb. 4:12). In the beginning, God commanded the earth to bring forth living things that reproduce after their kind. Life did not descend in a spaceship. It isn't an alien intruder. Matter is never lifeless. Life sprang from the earth itself, empowered by the Word and bursting with vigor and vitality. Despite all claims of tradition to the contrary, the undeniable Bible truth is that life is the fruit of the earth. The world is alive, and at God's command has given birth to all living creatures (Gen. 1:11-12, 24).

As God spoke, early in the first creation period, the earth awakened, rubbed her eyes, and excitedly began preparing for the new day. Eagerly she washed her face in the waters, and dressed herself with vegetation. Then God commanded the waters to teem with living creatures, and the splashing waters joyfully brought forth the living creature. He commanded the earth to produce animals breathing the breath of life. And the earth said yes, and brought forth animals of the field, creeping things, and cattle after their kind. And God blessed them, and commanded them to reproduce, to be fruitful and multiply.

The Creator was highly pleased. All that he had made was good, exactly in accordance with his plans and purposes. And now he was just about ready for one last creation, the crowning work of the entire project. The earth would bring forth again.

Preparing for Christ

We mustn't imagine the primal world as a mythical utopia of moral perfection where all creatures great and small lived without strife. Eden was not Oz. There were already restless stirrings in Paradise. The laws and processes, the principalities and powers that God spoke at the start, have not changed. Competition and conflict were present when our world was young. Like today, struggle and death roamed everywhere. Lambs ate grass and lions ate lambs. The music of nature was played with cymbals as well as harps. Creation was in counterpoint, a harmony of conflict.

This world was intended to be only temporary. It was not meant for eternity. The separation between Spirit and Body would be repaired. To see this clearly, we must throw off the shroud of tradition and read the Bible in the clear light of Spirit-guided understanding. We must listen to the inner voice that speaks softly from its pages. We must have ears to hear. We must never wrongly confuse tradition and orthodoxy with truth.

Good and Pregnant

God's declaration that the creation was good does not mean it was morally perfect. It means simply that the creation was pleasing to the Creator. It was according to his will, exactly as he had intended. He could now see his Son prefigured within it (Ps. 139:13-16). The Father is ultimately only well-pleased in the Son (Matt. 3:17). He finds joy and gladness in the child of his good pleasure. The world was good, not because of its supposed moral qualities, but because it pleased its Creator. It was exactly as he had wished. His plans and desires were being fulfilled in ever new and delightful ways that gave him immense joy. And it would all lead one day to the child of his delight.

The creation was truly magnificent. God was totally pleased. The world had turned out just the way he had imagined it should. The Word knew exactly what the Creator wanted, that which was pleasing to the august Author of all existence. Because the world was altogether pleasing to the Creator, it was good. And it was pregnant.

Understanding Good and Evil

We must clearly understand the scriptural viewpoint here. Good is not that which benefits humans. Nor is evil that which hurts humans. The ultimate quality and character of an action doesn't depend on its effect on us. That false, humanistic notion is rooted in pride and watered by arrogance. We must uproot it with the sharp spade of truth. Human welfare is not the standard of right and wrong.

Good is whatever pleases God, whatever is in harmony with his will. Evil is whatever opposes his will. The creation was good because it pleased the Creator. It was alive, abounding with possibilities, and one day would give birth to his beloved Son. In Adam, God could see the reflection of himself, and of his coming child. This pleased him greatly. With the coming of Adam and Eve, the world was very good!

Whispers of the Son

Yes, when he created Adam and Eve, the world was not merely good, it was very good. In them, God could clearly see his Son taking form in the womb of creation. They would be the progenitors of

God's Firstborn. The Father's joy and anticipation were unbounded. He was intensely pleased with the world's progress. The Word was doing a good job. Things were moving along exactly as God had desired. His plans were taking form. God's dream was coming true.

The creation of Adam was through the natural processes already established within the world. The world was forming according to the Word that was spoken from the beginning. The earth was bringing forth the living creature. It was not a disruption of the normal flow of natural events. The Word was moving in the processes of nature, a master artisan scooping up handfuls of clay and molding them into all sorts of curious creatures that lived and breathed and reproduced, all according to their kinds.

The breath of life was everywhere, bustling with energy and activity (Eze. 37:1-10). One of these living creatures formed from the earth was named Adam. Adam shared the same breath of life as the other animals (Gen. 2:7, 6:17, 7:15, 22). Contrary to tradition, he did not have uniquely within him an immortal soul. He was the highest of the living creatures that God had made (Gen. 1:20, 24, 2:7). And like them, he was born to die (Ps. 49:12, 20; Eccl. 3:18). He was made in the image of God. The creation whispered excitedly of the future, foreshadowing the Son. And God was watching closely, smiling at the resemblance.

This primal man was made in God's likeness, an archetype prefiguring the Son of God and the Creator's eternal purposes. The world was alive, bursting with possibilities, energized by the Spirit of God and obedient to the Word of his power. And it held clearly within its womb the man Jesus, who would be the very essence of God's Word and will. Oh, the wonder of it all! Heaven waited breathlessly, and the earth groaned with anticipation. When would it happen?

Right On Time

Let's jump forward to a small village in Palestine, to a stable where a humble carpenter and his wife have settled in for the night. But step softly, or you'll awaken the baby! Look there, in the manger. The tiny one sleeps. Now, after so many long eons, after the slow, careful work of the Word in the world, the moment has arrived. A Jewish virgin has given birth to a boy child! Heaven's joy is beyond description. Angels shout and sing God's highest glories, announcing this long-awaited birth. God looks in, and smiles. He is pleased with the world (Luke 2:8-14).

Born into the world, Jesus was fully a part of it, the very embodiment of God's will. He was the best work of the Word that eons earlier had formed the world, the top of the line. That same Word now carefully worked the earth into human form once more, carefully, intricately, in a special way. Now at last, in the slow, methodical march of days had come a special human baby, a virgin-born Israelite, heaven's joy and earth's delight.

The Spirit who once moved merrily over the primordial deep has never totally left the world, but moves invisibly within it, coaxing, tugging. God's Spirit-imbued Word has guided the creation from the start (Gen. 1:1-3). Unerringly, with the passage of the many carefully counted days, it has led the world to this lowly stable in Bethlehem.

God's Other Sons

For empowering Mary to conceive and give birth, God could be called Jesus' Father. But his true fatherhood would await Jesus' future baptism. Then heaven's voice could declare openly, "You are my Son, the beloved" (Ps. 2:7; Luke 3:22). God became the true Father of Christ Jesus on a bank of the Jordan. Jesus' Sonship and God's Fatherhood were not co-eternal. The idea of co-eternal, unchanging Father and Son is unbiblical, totally illogical, and impossible. It's an attempt to cover the nakedness of a three-headed idol. But it won't work. It's much too small. Look away, child.

Sonship and fatherhood cannot be static. Time must pass. A timeless process is a contradiction in terms. It's like calling the picture of a horserace a race. The horses don't actually run. There's no action, no change, and no movement. It isn't a real race. An unmoving race is nonsense. Likewise, generation can't be instantaneous. Time must pass. And in the process, God has changed. The Creator has become the Father, and a Son has come into being. A result can never be co-eternal with its cause. A son can never be the same age as his father. And unchanging generation is nonsense. It's blather. Don't believe it, child.

In the beginning was the Word. God expressed the world into being. It was a process. Speaking takes time. In time, the same divine Word brought forth flesh, human flesh. God was changing. Metamorphosis is the very purpose and character of creation, and the very heart of the Gospel. Christ Jesus, being the Son and Heir, will inherit all that pertains to God. All that God is, will be realized and manifested in Christ.

Yes, the angel said that Jesus would be called the Son of God. But every Jew claimed God as heavenly Father (Matt. 5:16; Mark 11:25; Luke 11:2, John 8:41, etc.). The nation of Israel, each and every male, was God's firstborn son, not because God had impregnated every Jewish mother, but because he had orchestrated the events of Israel's birth (Exod. 4:22). His fatherhood of Israel was figurative. Likewise, Jesus would be called God's Son not because God impregnated Mary, but because God had orchestrated the events of his birth. Israel's birth and sonship foreshadowed that of Jesus. And Jesus' birth prefigured and foreshadowed his new birth that would soon arrive, a short thirty years later.

After the cross he was given the name above all names, exalted to the throne of highest majesty as an example for every believer who receives the same Christ Spirit. In Spirit baptism all believers become born-again Children of God, begotten of the Father, and are co-inheritors with Christ (John 17:14-16, 18, 21-24; Rom. 8:17-21; 1 Cor. 3:21-23; 1 John 3:1-2, 4:4-6; 2 Peter 1:4, etc.). They will inherit the same oneness which Father and Son now enjoy (John 17:21-23). Jesus is firstborn among many (Heb. 2:10-13). They're like him. He has lots of brothers and sisters. And we all have one Father.

This is the Gospel promise, and the secure and certain birthright of every saint. We look forward to re-assimilation into the inner being of the Creator, the reunion of Body and Spirit. The joy of salvation is not a look backward, or a staid and stodgy repetition of this present world. It's an exaltation into an infinitely more glorious existence within the exquisite glory of God himself. The saints will follow Jesus all the way to glory, and beyond.

Death by Design

Begotten by the Spirit's influence, Jesus was yet a product of the earth. He was God's Word fulfilling God's will through the natural laws and processes of the creation. The principalities and powers of this world were at work in him, just as they are in every other human. He lived within the natural flow of the creation, growing slowly to maturity like every human. His growth and nourishment came from the earth, from the productive, fertile soil.

His body, like that of every other human, grew by assimilating to itself the living planet. He was human in the fullest sense. Mary's baby was human like her, and like you and I.

As he grew into manhood the original Word spoken at the creation continued to fulfill itself and become real. In Jesus, as in every other human, it was a lifelong process that continued past his birth into the whole course of his growth into adulthood. Like every other human, every time he ate a meal, or drank a cup of water, the Word was being fulfilled, becoming real, fulfilling the originating words of creation. This special embodiment of the originating Word spoken in Eden continued throughout the thirty-three years of his life. And yet, at his birth there was an even greater fulfillment of the Word waiting, a greater birth (John 1:14).

It would happen as he emerged, dripping wet, from the Jordan's waters, foreshadowing his future. A cross was waiting. But it would not be the end. It would be a new beginning, for him and for the creation. Resurrection and exaltation beckoned from beyond death, smiling encouragingly, lovingly. Jesus took that flesh, transformed, into the heavenly glory. What a stupendous honor God was preparing for the world!

In Bethlehem's Babe, the divine Word that had formed the world in the beginning now did his best work. But wonder of wonders! This special one, the highest of all God's handiwork would die like all other humans! This wasn't a new twist in the plot of history. From the start, God's plan included the death of his Son. The Son would be made in his own image. In God's surprising, stunning course determined beforehand in the counsels of eternity, the creation had become the man from Galilee in order that he too, like all other men and like God himself, should die, in order to rise unto greater glory.

Jesus' birth and death were planned from the beginning. Being of the earth, carried along by the ever-flowing current of time and place, he too was subject to the law of temporality and impermanence. All the things of this world must end. When impermanence applies to living beings, it is called death. Jesus, like the rest of the creation, was subject to the law of temporality. A cross was waiting among the trees, growing, biding its time.

The laws and processes of nature, the principalities and powers, will fulfill God's purposes. This world, from its inception, was meant to be only temporary, just an inkling of the glorious life that awaits beyond the clouds. Death was a principle established by God in the beginning, to effect the temporariness of human and other life. Death was part of God's plan of metamorphosis. He did not fear it. He commanded it. Death was his servant. Like Father like Son. Jesus would be the exact image of the Creator, and die. But he would be resurrected as well, like his Father.

Death would finish its grim work assigned to it. But it could not conquer, or continue forever. The wild horse of freedom would be tamed and ridden by its true Master. The stouthearted Son of God would mount this wild steed and ride deep into the blackest shades of awful night. Death would enfold the Son within its clammy embrace. But it would not be able to hold him. Death for the Son would be just a temporary separation of Spirit from Body. Reconciliation would come quickly, in three short days. The gates of Hell would be opened from the inside, unhinged forever. Life would be let loose into the open, flowered fields of eternity.

In the beginning, all the principalities and powers placed in the world by the Creator to accomplish his plan came to attention and began their service of separation. Death was one of them, mingling with the crowd. When the dance started he was there, laughing, shaking hands with everyone, learning everyone's name, inviting them to leave the dance and go outside with him.

Death is not a party crasher. He's an invited guest, one of the first to arrive. When the music of creation began, he quickly took to the dance floor, and showed himself to be a skillful, untiring dancer. And he always chose partners from among the living beings. Death has ever danced with life. He knows all the dance steps. But now, with the arrival of Jesus, Death has chosen the wrong partner!

With the arrival of the one chosen to become the true Son, things are about to change. This is the moment for which all the laws and processes have been preparing for eons, honing their abilities, practicing their skills over and over. Death struts among them, boastful and confident. Now, at center stage and with all of heaven in attendance, the principalities and powers must do their very best, for the Creator is in the audience, watching.

Chapter TWO

A Beginning with Promise

From God's Bleeding Side

Spoken, written, or enacted, the word of God still holds unimaginably potent power and dynamism. It is God's expression inspired with divinity, infused with the Spirit (2 Tim. 3:16). And he speaks, surprisingly, in the events of history. The world itself is the product of God's expression, the fulfillment of his word (Ps. 19:1-6; 2 Peter 3:5). The laws and processes of creation, and the things that happen, reveal him. This is especially clear in the events recorded in the Bible, the word there being more fine-tuned and focused, translated into human language so that one day his children could read it. Like a spoken prophecy, the Bible history is God's Spirit-filled word jumping up and down and speaking excitedly of even greater and more marvelous things to come. It grabs us by the hand and pulls us toward a brighter future beyond the clouds.

It tells of Christ, even from the beginning. Through his word, God expresses himself. The word of God is his self-revelation, and it focuses on Christ. Did you get that? In his word, God expresses himself, to reveal Christ. And this world is the result of God's self-expression. Do you see the connection? The goal and destiny of this world is Christ in his fullness. And that fullness will be the embodiment of God. In the fullness of Christ, God's Body will be reconstituted.

The beginning is a foreshadowing, God's promise of the future, of wonders yet to come. The creation of the world, and especially of Adam and Eve, tells of a coming world that will be much greater and more marvelous than the present. This world speaks excitedly of the next one. It urges us to Christ, God's living Word fulfilled, the very image of God. He is its theme and purpose, its promise and its realization. He is the firstborn of the new creation that is forming all around us. The earth has a glorious future awaiting it.

It had a glorious past as well. It came from God, literally. Indeed, it was God.

Not From Nothing

Contrary to much misguided religious tradition, the world did not originate magically from nothingness. Toss the shroud aside, child. And don't let its dust get in your eyes. The act of creation is a process of bringing into existence things that do not yet exist. It's a process, not a magic trick. Existence is a becoming. It is never stationary or stagnant. It does not originate from emptiness, but from prior things, always, in constant movement and change. Creation is a river that never runs dry, because it issues from the throne of God.

It flows in time and space (Isa. 43:7, 45:7, 12, 18). This is the plain teaching of the Scriptures, and the clear evidence of experience. The future springs from the present. Every moment flows into the next. This world will birth the next one. Creation is the continuing transformation into something new of that which already exists. Creation is change. It's metamorphosis. And God is the Creator.

Surprisingly for many traditionalists, the Bible is actually quite specific about the meaning of creation. Adam was created from the dust of the earth. And Eve was created from Adam's side. They didn't suddenly jump out of a divine magic hat. Creation is not a parlor trick. The world was not birthed from nothingness, but from God (1 Cor. 11:12). It's not just the work of his hands, it's the rib from his side, so to speak. The new creation, too, will arise from this present world, not from nil. There is no verse in the Bible that says creation is from nothing.

History is the story that God is telling, a thrilling and exciting drama complete with noble heroes and rascally villains. Events are his words, moving the suspenseful plot forward toward its surprising and unexpected climax. In the story of the world, the vicious, fearsome beast of evil rampages everywhere, seemingly invincible, ready to swallow up all that's good and gracious. Things look bleak. Everything will be destroyed. But look, here's heaven's hero, come to do battle with the ferocious beast.

But oh, dear. Heaven's hero is a lamb! A lamb? It's lamb against dragon. And the lamb is slain!

Let not your heart be troubled, little one. God is the author of history. As he speaks, the future takes form. Events line up and await their turn. That which exists gives birth to that which does not yet exist. The creation itself tells of this incredible wonder if we listen closely, and if we recognize the clues, for it too is God's word (Ps. 19:1-6). It has purpose, God's purpose. And that purpose is Christ. History, too, is the revelation of God. And his full revelation will be Christ.

And child, we will be revealed with him, sharing in his glory (Col. 3:4, 1 John 3:2)!

This world is a river continuously flowing, a process of evolving, a story still being told. The Bible helps us understand its language and interpret what it says. When we politely ask where the world came from, the Bible smiles and points to God. When we ask where it is going, the Bible again smiles and points to God.

Events come to life as the expression of the very Spirit of life, from that ever-flowing fountain that erupts from the throne of God and infuses his word with himself. The Bible says that in the beginning, the Word was with God and the Word was God. And as God expressed himself, the world was formed. It was according to God's will (John 1:3-4).

And in an astounding turn of events, in obedience to the word, life arose. It sprang from the earth itself, not as an infusion of something alien from the outside, but as an expression of God himself. God speaks in the wonders of nature (Ps. 19:1-6; Rom. 1:20). We must listen, as God's still, small voice whispers of the world's origination from himself, and as it speaks eagerly of its wondrous future. It will tell us of the long-awaited and sure to come fullness of the Son.

Imaging God

As we look where he tells us, we can see Adam and Eve hiding there behind the trees, blushing and embarrassed. See them there, hiding? If we ask them to come out and tell us what they're doing, they shyly point away from themselves to God. They're imaging God, they say. They are portraying the Creator, the Archetype, coming together again into one flesh (Gen. 1:26-27). That seems strange, doesn't it?

But it's true. The image is not something divine in their biological makeup. The image of God does not reside in human DNA, any more than in the DNA of monkeys or elephants. Adam and Eve were not two little idols, child. They were not images of God. They were made in his image. There's a world of difference between imaging and being an image. One is worship, while the other is idolatry.

His image is the manner in which they were created, and the role they played. Their creation echoed the creation of the world itself, pointing reverently back to the Creator, and forward to his metamorphosis. It was a three-paned mirror, a triptych imaging past, present, and future. Their initial separation followed by their coming together again as one flesh was a word about God past, present, and future. They were images of an even greater couple to come. There would be a greater Adam in a greater Eden, and a greater Eve (1 Cor. 15: 20-22, 45).

The manner of their creation tells us something extremely important about God and creation. It points to the source, purpose, and goal of this world. It reveals something of the world's destiny, and our place in it. Yes, Adam and Eve were created, but they didn't arise from nothingness, did they? Eve's extraction from Adam imaged the extraction of the world from its Creator. Like Eve, the world did not originate from nothingness. Eve was a figure of the coming Church, the Body of God (Eph. 5:31-32). The Church, too, like Eve, is not created from nothingness. Adam, prefiguring the greater Adam, likewise is not a product of zero, but of the living earth (1 Cor. 15:45). Zero multiplied by any number, however large, is still zero. Nothing can come from nothing. This world came from God's rib, so to speak. It issued from God.

A Bride for the Creator

To traditionalists, the world's origination from the substance of God is a startling idea, like a ghost that suddenly materializes. It goes against church tradition. Christians have imagined that God's utter holiness means that he is wholly Spirit, wholly other and different from this world, a wholly holy ghost. His holiness has pushed God out of his own creation. The traditional, unscriptural doctrine of *creatio ex nihilo*, creation from nothing, cavorts insanely everywhere. Christians have been taught this doctrine for centuries. But it's not what the Bible teaches. The Bible urgently and emphatically tells us that God and embodiedness are not at all incompatible.

It proudly presents to us the incarnation of Christ Jesus, the God-man, in bold red letters, underlined and capitalized. It reaches out to us fervently and tells us of the physical, bodily resurrection of Jesus through his physical, bodily oneness with the Spirit.

He lives eternally as One with God, in an embodied manner. At the center of the Bible and the Christian faith is an empty tomb, because he took human flesh, transformed, into the heavenly glory. Embodiedness is not at all incompatible with God's being, then, or with eternity. The unscriptural idea of creation from nothing illogically denies God's past embodiedness while opening its arms wide to a greatly anticipated bodily resurrection with Christ. Huh? Does that make sense?

To push God totally outside of his creation erases every page of Scripture. It denies the entire Bible and ignores Christ Jesus. God has always been intimately involved in the world. Creation was its temporary, partial separation from him, imaged by the creation of Eve from Adam. The image of God in them was the testimony that their creation gave. It was Eve's temporary separation from Adam in order to transform her and bring her back to him, to be re-united into one new flesh. Their story imaged the separation of the world from God and its loving reconciliation back to him in the Body of Christ (Gen. 2:22-24). The Bible centers on salvation, which is the Spirit and Body coming together again, forever.

Adam was put to sleep, a figure of death, a typology. God then created Eve from his side, to complete him and chase away his solitude. In their mutual love and life together, the two would become one flesh (Gen. 2:24). These events testified of future wonders. Jesus too, the true image of God, would be put to sleep, and from that sleep of death God would create a Bride for him, a helpmeet. The two would become one Body. And Christ is the true image of God, a trustworthy representation of the Creator.

Adam was a figure of Christ. Like Jesus, Adam's side was pierced while he slept. He shed his blood for his bride. The greater Adam's side was pierced while he slept too, by a Roman spear. From the blood and water that flowed, a symbol of his life, God is creating a Bride for the Son, just as earlier he had created a bride for Adam. Both events told about death, but also of new life. The creation and marriage of Adam and Eve speak expectantly and approvingly of the new creation and the coming marriage of the Lamb.

Biblical marriage is a joining, a uniting into oneness. The world's separation from God, then, like Eve's separation from Adam, was not absolute. The creation was designed so that the Word of God could in time become joined with human flesh, and the world could be reconciled and reunited back to God in Christ. Christ's marriage, still future, was God's ultimate purpose for creation, foreshadowed in Eden (Col. 1:19-20). The marriage of Christ is the reason for the world, the complete fulfillment of God's Word in the fullness of Christ. This Word is still echoing. And God is listening and watching. He's waiting eagerly for his Bride to be fully formed.

Eve's temporary separation from Adam, imaging the world's separation from God, was only until she was ready for oneness. At the proper time she would be brought back to him, and they would be together again, one flesh, once more.

Eve's creation from Adam, involving her temporary separation from him, would be the delightful answer to Adam's original solitude. Likewise, the world's temporary separation from God was just a preliminary step. God will find immense new joy and gladness in his new Bride.

Pictures that Point

It's clearly evident that God has expressed himself in the creation. His presence is everywhere. His voice can still be heard in the blowing of the winds, calling out to anyone with ears to hear. But his intents and purposes pulsate with a beat far longer than human lifetimes. So he has patiently spoken to us through seers and prophets, and has carefully provided us the Scriptures. His word draws us to himself and his long-range purposes, and calls us to join with him in their accomplishment. He has drawn word pictures and object lessons for us in its pages, revealing himself and his goals. He's an Artist, and he draws pictures of himself; past, present, and future.

The Law of Moses

One of these word pictures is the Mosaic Law given to Israel. Arriving awesomely with pomp and ceremony, the Law was nevertheless just a series of preliminary drawings on the chalkboard of history. In the Law, the divine Teacher was illustrating his long-range will and purposes (Heb. 8:5, 10:1). It was a preview of coming attractions. He drew happy pictures of things that are in harmony with his long-term will, and labeled them righteousness. And he made dark, ugly drawings of things that work against his long-term will, and called them sins. Sinfulness and righteousness in the Law are not absolutes, however. They're just preliminary sketches of something greater that would soon come.

Once more, we must jerk the shroud of tradition rudely away so that we can see the truth. Sin and righteousness are just illustrations, line drawings that the divine Teacher drew on the chalkboard, figures of a reality beyond themselves. When the lesson was over, the divine Teacher erased them. He erased the Law, and with it, sin.

Sins are transgressions of the Law, dirty, ugly things that cringe and hide in fear of a greater darkness beyond themselves (1 John 3:4). When we politely ask of them their meaning, they shrink back uneasily, avoiding eye contact, and slightly nod their heads toward their looming fulfillment, the outer darkness outside of Christ.

Sins are law's children, and they never leave her side. They hang onto her skirts like a baby possum hangs onto its mother. They cannot live apart from the law. Apart from her they die, for sins are the breaking of the law. Where there's no law, there's no transgression, for if law doesn't exist, it can't be broken (Rom. 4:15). Surprising? Yes, sins draw their life from Law (1 Cor. 15:56). When Jesus erased the Law, he erased sins as well. It was release for all those who were under the Law. Its shackles were replaced by God's grace, love, and mercy (Gal. 5:13, 18). These are all included in what is called salvation. It's what the Gospel is all about.

Righteousness works similarly. It promises blessings and rewards, the consequences of keeping the Law. But if we ask about its meaning, it bows its head and it, too, humbly points away, to its fulfillment in Christ. Sin and righteousness are brothers, like Ishmael and Isaac, or Esau and Jacob. They both cling tightly to mother Law. Apart from the Law, righteousness cannot exist. Obedience of a law disappears when there is no law to obey. When Jesus erased the Law, works righteousness ceased to exist too. Sin and righteousness were but shadows, as was the Law itself. Yes, the Law and her children were just shadows, just stick figures. And they were only over Israel (Eph. 2:11-12).

The figures illustrate God's long-term purposes. True sin, the outer and utter darkness which sins in the Law tremblingly foreshadow, is separation from God, which results in eternal death. The dazzling, resplendent brightness which righteousness in the Law foreshadows is the safety and blessedness of being in Christ and no longer separated from God. Being in Christ brings eternal life and glory. The Law, with its issues of sin and righteousness, together with punishment or blessings, illustrates being inside or outside of Christ (Gal. 3:24). When the lesson of Law is done, its pictures are erased. They're just illustrations of God's purposes to be accomplished in Christ. And they were never over the Gentiles.

The Bible clearly teaches that there never was any true righteousness based on the Law. Neither, then, was there any true sinfulness. Yes, these were merely shadows of the truth beyond them. The whole concept of justice, of life based on legalism, is just another chalk drawing hanging onto mother Law. Justice is life based on Law. It, too, vanished when the Law was erased.

It's hard to imagine, programmed as we are to think that law and justice are real and right and good, but the Bible teaches that there will be no justice in heaven. The Law cannot enter past heaven's gates. Moses must die on Mt. Nebo, looking longingly across the Jordan, but unable to cross over.

Yes, surprisingly, justice and fairness, derived from Law, will not roam heaven's streets. God's unbounded and cleansing love will wash over everything and everyone. Great, towering tsunamis of grace and mercy will surge and flow freely everywhere. Salvation will flood earth and heaven.

There's no justice here on earth either. This world was not meant to be just. And it isn't, is it? Time and chance happen to everyone. Death roams everywhere, devilishly arbitrary and capricious. He lurks on every street corner, in every dark alley, ready to jump out and rob people of their lives. But he hides in the halls of so-called justice too.

Things like murder, idolatry, and robbery derive their label from law. They are sins only because the law says so. They acquired the character of sinfulness when the Law labeled them sins and forbade them. Apart from the Law, they were not sins, because sin is the breaking of the Law (1 John 3:4).

Actually, sin has no substantive reality. Sin is just an idea in the minds of people who imagine that a law exists and is broken. But an idea can't actually be broken. Think, child. If a law doesn't exist, if it's just an idea, it can't be broken, and it can't be kept. Doesn't that make sense? Both sin and righteousness only exist where there is law. And law is just an agreed-to cluster of communal ideas. And ideas can't be broken, or kept. Try it, and see for yourself. Find one, and then hit it with a hammer. See if it breaks. Or, perhaps you can catch one and keep it in your purse, or in a pot on the stove? No, the breaking and keeping of laws are just figures of speech. And laws themselves, all of them, are just communal ideas, written down of course.

The Mosaic Law is just a list of ideas with the purpose of pointing people to the truth. And the truth is Christ Jesus, who is the perfect embodiment of God's will, and the fulfillment of all the promises of the Law. All the Law, yes, including the Ten Commandments, was just a series of shadows fulfilled in Christ. None of those prefigurings was forever. In the meantime there was Israel, pointing to true Israel. There was manna, prefiguring the true Bread from heaven. And there was sin, and true sin. There were types, and their fulfillment or antitype.

The true sin toward which sins in the Law point is separation from Christ, which is separation from God. It brings eternal death. True righteousness is reconciliation with God, brought about by receiving Christ, which brings eternal life. These two concepts of true sin and true righteousness are prefigured in the Law. They were prefigured even earlier by what we call good and evil. These, too, are Law's children. They were brought to light with the first law in Eden when God commanded Adam to abstain from the tree of knowledge of good and evil, on pain of death. You know the story. He didn't abstain.

The Eye Opener in Eden

Contrary to tradition, that first law was not meant to give Adam moral freedom. A command that restricts freedom does not create it. It reflects it. It presupposes it. That first law, like every law, carried with it the possibility of disobedience. Obedience and disobedience are presupposed in laws. It's built-in to them. A law prohibiting an impossibility would not include the possibility of disobedience, and would make no sense whatever. It would be like prohibiting people from dying under 200 years of age. It could never be obeyed. The law in Eden implied that Adam could choose to obey or disobey.

Even here, at the beginning, God was hinting strongly, commandingly, that Adam was free. He was not a robot. Before the law, Adam already lived in total moral freedom. There were no restrictions on his conduct. Can you imagine that? The law then added accountability to his moral freedom. He didn't eat from the tree of freedom, but from the tree of knowledge, of good and evil.

And unexpectedly, before Adam was given that first law, there was no sin. He was like the other animals, having no concept of good and evil. The couple's being naked and unashamed shows that they were spiritually blind, and unaware of their condition. Like babies, they had no idea of right and wrong. They had no compass, no road map outside of themselves. This is the reason why God, in his lovingkindness, gave them that first law in the garden. It was to lift them above the other beasts.

It awakened their capacity for abstract thinking, and for planning and dreaming, and working toward those dreams. Even today, this ability is what helps us stand above the other beasts of the jungle. It puts us at the top of the food chain. It allows us to build civilizations, and religions, and churches. The important thing, though, is that obeying God's law meant doing his will.

Their inability to keep it opened their eyes to the nature of their humanity. It was selfish and inward-looking, ever bent on doing their own desires. When they disobeyed the law, they came to realize that their own will was antagonistic to God's will. Their eyes were opened to the concept of good and evil, good being God's will and evil being that which is contrary to it (Rom. 7:9). Their human nature was not capable of doing God's will. They were self-centered. The law was a can opener that showed them the worms inside of themselves. Death was already working in them, gnawing at their innards.

Eden's lesson is that carnal humanity is incapable of doing God's will. It's what the Law reveals. This is the basic human problem. God wants us to do his will, but our human nature makes us incapable of it. It's the reason why we must die. Our human nature is bent on doing our own desires rather than God's will. We need to be changed, and given a new heart. We need Christ. But we need to be shown that we need Christ. That's the function of God's Law. It's like an X-ray. It shows us what's inside of us. And it's not very pretty.

Every baby goes through this same process of having its eyes opened. During infancy, law doesn't exist for them. Then, as each child learns the rules of right and wrong conduct, of good and bad behavior, they acquire the concept of good and evil. When they break the rules, as every child does, they realize their guiltiness. They come to know their shortcomings, and become accountable, and apprehensive of getting caught. That's what law does. It finds you guilty. It opens your eyes to your true nature and character. Law is a mirror. If you look in it, you'll see yourself. And it's not very pretty.

This universal realization of personal responsibility and liability is not a fall from perfection. It's an upward step. When babies learn how to behave properly, it is not a fall, or a step backward. Potty training is good for all of us. And it's not a fall. Learning the rules is a step forward and upward. Law opens our eyes to the human predicament, just like it did in Eden. By looking in the mirror we can wash, and shave, and comb our hair, and see how our clothes fit.

Every society and culture has laws to govern behavior. And in every society, the existence of laws implies our human capacity to obey or disobey. They show that we are free to choose. The capacity to distinguish between good and evil is universal, and coincides with our God-given freedom. Freedom and responsibility go hand in hand. But laws can never take away our freedom. On the contrary, laws imply freedom. Even the most oppressive ones do. Without the ability to obey or disobey, laws make no sense whatever. Eden's law implied Adam's freedom.

When God gave Adam and Eve the first law and they disobeyed, it opened their eyes. Nowhere does the Bible say that they fell from perfection. There was no Fall of Man!

That's right, child. Forget the tradition. Eating did not magically change them, and the whole creation, from one state to another. Adam and Eve transgressed because of what they already were before they broke that first law. They were already covetous and curious, and self-centered. Their human nature was already what it is today (Rom. 8:7). Their sin was the expression of their already sinful nature, just as our own sin is the expression of our own sinful nature. You do what you are. Always. It's impossible to do otherwise (Matt. 15:19).

Law manifests our need to be reconciled to God in Christ. Adam and Eve, in their humanity, in their createdness, were not in harmony with that eternal purpose. They were self-oriented. The principality called Satan, along with death and temporality, were already working in them. They were animals, humans estranged from God, trapped in the temporariness of this world and unable to free themselves. They needed to be re-clothed (Col. 3:9-10). They needed help. They needed a Savior. The law opened their eyes to their distressing predicament.

That's what God's Law does. It discloses our sin and selfishness, and our need of Christ (Gal. 3:24). When someone hears the Spirit's convicting word, child, it's not a fall from perfection. No, it's an invitation to receive perfection. There was no fall in Eden. When the Spirit spoke to them, it wasn't to put a stumblingblock in their way (Lev. 19:14). It was to open their eyes. And it did.

God kindly clothed them in animal skins, then, in accord with their nature and their spiritual nakedness. They needed clothes (Gal. 3:27). The skins were prefigurative of the Incarnation. Jacob, a figure of Christ and the Incarnation, donned goatskins in order to gain the birthright (Gen. 27:1-29). Later the tabernacle, symbol of the Body of Christ, was covered with goatskins as well (Gen. 26:7). Goats and lambs were figures of Christ in his humanity (Lev. 1:10). This first couple's clothing pointed to him. God was already preaching the Gospel in Eden. Adam and Eve, and later all their children, needed to be clothed with Christ.

A perfect circle is never square. A square is never round. Dogs don't fly, and birds don't bark. And a perfectly moral being does not sin. But Adam and Eve sinned. What does that tell us about them? Eve ate the forbidden fruit because coveting was already part of her nature. Sin does not magically make a person a sinner. A person sins because sin already lurks within the person's heart (Mark 7:21-23). Sins are the expression of what we are. We do what we are. It's impossible to do otherwise. When Adam and Eve disobeyed, they were merely fulfilling the desires already yearning and burning inside (Gen. 3:6; Jas. 1:14-15).

The problem was that, in their carnal nature, they were incapable of doing God's will. They were unsuitable for serving as his Body. The Creator of course desired a Body that would serve him. Their very humanity was at odds with his long-range plans.

Humans were just the first step. They must die, and give place to something better.

No Fall in the Garden

The shroud of tradition lies everywhere in Christian doctrine, so let's repeat here the scriptural truth that their disobedience was not a trip and fall. Eve was not Clementine who stubbed her toe upon a splinter. The Scripture doesn't say their knees were skinned, or that their nature changed. It tells us that their eyes were opened (Rom. 7:7-9). Yes, the eyes of the blind were opened in Eden. They realized that they were dancing with Death, and he was holding them much too closely. The Law was a mirror (Rom. 3:20, 5:13). They looked at themselves and saw their spiritual state. So they clothed themselves with fig leaves. They saw themselves just as they were, spiritually naked and exposed. And this was actually a good thing.

How sad it would be if humans were to be deprived of spiritual sight! We would be like the other beasts, not knowing good and evil, like Adam before the law. Thankfully, the new creation will not be a return to Eden. In the true and greater Paradise, we'll not romp in the grass naked and unaware like babies or beasts, with no concept of right and wrong and no spiritual discernment! Our hearts and our destinies are not back in Eden, but in the New Jerusalem. There, in the halls of decency and decorum, we will be fully clothed with the pure, white linen of the Christ nature. We will be like God!

Thankfully, Jesus walked with his eyes open. He knew right from wrong, perfectly. He exercised the utmost spiritual discernment. And he's our ideal, our leader and example (Heb. 5:14). We strive to be like him. The desire to be like God, to know right from wrong, is not evil. Humankind's highest and noblest goal is godliness. The desire to be like God becomes evil only when it pretends godliness on its own terms, apart from the Spirit's enabling work. Then it is mere imitation, an act of pretense and pride. Such imitation of God is satanic, child. Don't do it. To be godly, let Christ Jesus be himself inside you. It's the only way.

The Sin of Imitating God

Satan longs to be like God. He imitates God, but rejects Christ. But Christ, only Christ, is the true image and expression of God (2 Cor. 4:4; Col. 1:15). Did you get that? Adam and Eve, in their carnality, being just types, can only point away from themselves to him. The manner of their creation, and their relationship to one another, is the image of God. The image is not in their human nature. Human nature is a snake pit. It's where the Serpent lives. He lives in the human heart.

However much he imitates, the Serpent can never be the Savior. He can only pretend. The human pretense to image God is in reality imitation of Satan! Any image of God other than Christ within the human breast is an idol! Don't be fooled, little one. God's image in Adam was his typological function. There was nothing in his physical or spiritual makeup that was the image of God. Don't make Adam, and everyone else, into an idol, into an image of God as the tradition so wrongly does.

However, God's desire and intent in the beginning was indeed to form humans in his image. He has not changed his mind or wavered from that purpose. It's just that the former image is just a foreshadowing of his true, long-range intent. The fulfillment of the shadow image in Adam is Christ Jesus. Humans are made in the true image of God by receiving Christ (1 John 3:2). God wants us to be like him. To that end, he became like us (Heb. 2:14-18). The everlasting God underwent a change, and took on human form. Astounding, isn't it? In Christ, God is forming humans in his own image, to share in his dominion. But they must share his story too.

Sin Did Not Separate

The dust of tradition is flying everywhere, is it not? But let's keep pulling at the shroud. By the way, our quarrel is not with traditionalists. It's with the false traditions. Let's continue, and read the Bible and see that God has never lost touch with the world. Contrary to much empty-headed preaching, Adam and Eve's sin did not separate them from close fellowship with him. After their disobedience, God continued to speak with them as before.

God walked with Enoch, and spoke with Noah and Job, and with many other prophets. Abraham was God's friend. Moses spoke face to face with him. Repeatedly, God has manifested himself within the world and has kept up a relationship with humanity. He gave Israel the Law, and he gave the world Christ Jesus. Sin did not separate the world from God. The process of creation did. But it's not a spatial separation. It's a qualitative separation, a differentiation.

The tradition that Adam and Eve lost their earlier direct communication with God is just the figment of someone's wild imagination. It's just a dream told as if it were real, and received as if it had actually happened. To share the dream, listeners must fall asleep too. Don't fall asleep, child, especially in church. The Scriptures do not substantiate that Adam and Eve lost their former close communication with God. The first law, in Eden, opened their eyes. It didn't trip them or push them off a cliff into imperfection, or from communication with God. They neither fell, nor fell away. There was no cliff in Eden.

Think. How childish a notion it is, that humanity and indeed the entire creation could somehow fall from a pristine perfection just because Adam and Eve ate from a tree in a garden, even if it was a lemon. To fall from perfection is nonsense. It always raises the unanswerable question of the origin of evil. The notion holds as much truth as does Pandora's box. And you know how much truth that is? Zilch. Events in Eden were according to God's plan, envisioned even before the creation, and accomplished in a natural manner just as he had imagined.

Actions Are Not Inherited

It is equally childish to think that Adam's disobedience could somehow be transferred to his descendants. If your great, great, grandfather stole a horse, are you a horse thief? Should they hang you? Or, if he studied medicine, would you be born a doctor? No, actions can't be inherited. Guilt is not in our genes. Guilt comes from breaking the law, and only exists by hanging onto the law's skirts. It's just a picture on the chalkboard that's erased in Christ. It's just an idea, child, just an idea. If we inherit the sins of our ancestors, you not only inherit Adam's sin, but you also inherit every single sin that your ancestors have committed, all the way back to Adam! My, how guilty you must be!

Moreover, if sin is inherited, then Jesus was guilty of Adam's sin too. After all, he too was a descendant of Adam and son of Mary (Luke 3:38). So then, he was guilty, like you, of the sins of all his ancestors. How could he be counted sinless, then?

But we aren't guilty of Adam's disobedience. We're sinners because we share his nature. Are you human? If so, then you are separated from God and must die. Like Adam and Eve, you're part of this temporal creation, smack dab in the middle of it, deeper than your eyeballs. You're not guilty of Adam's disobedience, or that of your parents, but you must die because of your alienation from the Creator. That's the true sin of which sins under law whisper fearfully in hushed tones. They whisper about you!

Likewise, we're counted innocent, regardless of what we've done, when we receive the Spirit of Christ. This reconciles and reunites us with God, to share in his eternal, divine nature, no longer alienated from him in our createdness (1 Cor. 15:48-50). This is why salvation comes only by receiving Christ and the new birth. Receiving Christ frees us from the bear trap of this world. We must put on the new nature, through his Word (1 Peter 1:23). And receiving his Word is not just assenting intellectually to its truth. It means to literally receive it. The Word of God is Christ himself. We must receive Christ, and with him reunion with God.

Adam's disobedience was an action. Actions aren't inherited, child. There's no gene for right or wrong behavior, or for guilt. There's no guilt gene that can make you guilty for what your ancestors did. And there's no God gene that would make you an image of God. Adam's carnal, human nature is what we inherit. He disobeyed God by choosing to obey his own nature. That's what we love to do, too. We love the harsh taskmasters of Egypt, the principalities and powers that thrive in our humanity. That's one of the lessons of the Exodus.

We love, honor, and obey our inherited creatureliness, our carnality that participates in the creation alienated from God. Being in and of this world is what causes death, for this world is purposely temporary. It's just the prototype for a better one. Carnal man, part and parcel of this present world, will die so that the spiritual man might live. Had Adam not eaten the forbidden fruit, he still would have died. He needed to eat from the tree of life in order to live forever. He was mortal. Only God is immortal (1 Tim. 6:16). Yes, only God is immortal. And eternal life is only in Christ, not in Adam. Life in Adam is the same life in which all the animals share. And animals, even human animals, do not live forever.

The Big Picture

Clearly, if we are to understand God's purpose for the creation and for our lives, we must know the truth. Myths and magic will not help us understand God's plans. In order to bring our lives into harmony with God's will, we must understand what the Bible actually teaches, and receive it. Loyalty to orthodoxy is no help if that orthodoxy is false, even if it's heartfelt and sincere. Mere religion or tradition without truth is worse than worthless. Zeal in falsehood is folly. Only the truth can bring us into harmony with God's will and purpose. Loyalty to tradition or church is good only when these hold to the truth. When a church teaches falsehood or idolatry, however sincerely or passionately, we must let it go, reach for the truth, and hold on for dear life.

Createdness Is Separation

The truth is that the first sin in Eden did not cause this world to fall. That's a silly, magical idea. Neither did it separate Adam and Eve from God. Nor did it cause their condemnation. It was merely a product of the first law. It was just a shadow. Without that first law, their eating of the fruit would not have been sin, for the fruit would not have been forbidden. But they still would have died. In order to live forever, they needed to eat from the tree of life. They were already separated from God by their createdness, trapped in this temporal world. They hadn't realized their danger until they disobeyed the law, and their eyes of spiritual understanding were opened. When they saw their nakedness, it wasn't because they had fallen. It was because their eyes were opened. Law doesn't cause our alienation from God. It manifests it. Law is a flashlight.

Yes, it's true, as Paul says, that sin, and the realization of personal inadequacy, entered the world through Adam (Rom. 5:12). Sin and guilt were children of the first law, clinging to her skirts. Apart from that law, Adam could not have sinned. But his nature would still be what it is today. Eating a bite of fruit did not magically change his nature. Think, child. When you eat an apple do you fall? Do you turn into a monster? Neither did Adam. He was what he was. And we are what we are. We don't inherit his disobedience. We inherit his nature and his world. We inherit death. Death dances with everyone, and he never tires. And he knows everybody's name.

The Origin and Design of Death

Adam was the first sinner, so sin entered the world through him (Rom. 5:12-14). Because he was a sinner, oriented to self-service, he was unsuitable for serving in God's Body. So he was expulsed from Eden and barred from the tree of life. That's why he died. And all his children died as well, for they too were barred from the tree of life, because they too sinned. Their nature was like that of their father. They didn't sin like Adam, by disobeying God's prohibition, nor did they break any of the prohibitions in the Law of Moses, which came only much later. But they still died. What was their sin? What was the reason for their death?

It lay in the fact that their human nature was itself turned inward, oriented toward self-service, away from God. They did all those things that would later be prohibited by the Law of Moses. And even if these things were not imputed because the Law had not yet been given, they still died, for they were barred from the tree of life. Like their father, they were not suitable, in their humanity, for serving in God's living Temple. Their human nature itself was incapable of doing God's will. In their carnality, in their createdness, they were estranged from God.

They died because of their nature, which is self-oriented. Their death was not the result of breaking God's law. It was because of their humanity itself, which hides the Serpent inside of it. Law merely exposes the innate selfishness already present in the human heart. Disobedience manifests the human condition of self-oriented separation from God inherited from Adam, inherent in our createdness. Humans are naturally oriented toward self and begin dying even from birth. The Law of Moses, in the Spirit's power, opens our eyes to the dire urgency of our need.

Law, which creates morality, has spread to all Adam's seed (Rom. 2:12-16, 3:9, 23, 11:32). Every mother teaches her child right and wrong. And every child transgresses. But that act of disobedience usually does not cause death. Children don't automatically die when they reach the age of accountability, do they? The sinful, corruptible nature itself, from which the transgression arises, is the true cause of death. Babies die too!

It's likewise with animals. They don't die because their ancestor ate an apple, or even if they themselves eat one. Death is natural. Humans, like all the animals, hold the death principle within their very nature. We were made purposely temporal, and subject to the cycles that recur in this creation, to the principalities and powers that govern this world. We're all barred from the tree of life. We can't get past the cherubim that guard the way.

Death didn't invade the creation through Adam's disobedience. Disobedience doesn't create sinfulness. It's the other way around. Sinfulness creates disobedience. The Law was an intrusion into the natural workings of this world, to lead us eventually to Christ, who would be the annulment of this world's processes. Adam was not meant to live forever, because his nature was incapable of the obedience that God desires. That's what the law disclosed. Adam must evolve into Christ. A new birth was necessary. And it wasn't an afterthought.

It's worth repeating that events in Eden showed Adam that he was not suitable for service in God's eternal Body. His heart, like ours, was ever saying, "Not your will, but my will be done, and quickly." Self-will is at enmity with God's will (Rom. 8:5-13). Can the Body of God function correctly if its parts will not and cannot do what his mind wills? The saints are saved so that they can become members of the Body. Will the Body of God be paralyzed, or lame, or misshapen? No, if we are to be incorporated into his Body, we must be changed, and capacitated to do his will rather than our own. This is why we must receive Christ and be converted. It's why we must learn to do his will.

Sins are the result and expression of self-centeredness. Humans are selfs. Their intents and desires are inward and exclusionary. What is important is my life, my family, my friends, my team, my city, my country, my species. My, my, my, everything is about me.

This orientation toward self is one of the principalities that governs in this temporary creation, and is destined for destruction. Believers must learn to overcome the sinful, carnal life, and die to self. Selfishness must be doffed so that selflessness can be donned (1 Cor. 15:53-57). We must learn to serve God rather than self. Isn't this what Jesus taught? We must die, to be changed, to be resurrected to heavenly glory. God's will is our worshipful service.

To exist in this world necessarily means to partake of death. Everyone does it. It's the principality God uses to achieve our intended impermanence. He planned for it to work in everyone, and it does, but not forever. Adam was never immortal. And all his children inherit his mortality. Sorry.

However, in Christ Jesus eternal life is our generous portion. Death too, being part of this world, will go the way of all things temporal. It will be chased into oblivion.

We humans are not condemned for Adam and Eve's disobedience. It would be altogether unjust to punish one person for the sins of another, or to reward the guilty for someone else's righteousness (Rom. 2:6-11). We don't die for what Adam did, but rather for what we are. Death is built into our nature. But it's not a punishment for having broken the law. It's just the natural state. It's the way things are. The human animal, like all the others, was never meant to live forever.

We can't blame Adam and Eve for our problems. Had they not eaten of the tree we would still die, but in spiritual blindness like the other animals. Death was not produced by their transgression, but by what their transgression of the law manifested, which is the death principle inherent in the world because of its orientation away from God. This world will be destroyed so that a new, brighter world can rise from its ashes (Rom. 6:6-11; Eph. 4:22-24). From the beginning, this natural world has pulled wildly away from God and life (John 3:18). Persons who refuse to join their destiny with the eternal will and purpose of God remain wild and alienated. They seal their death along with the rest of the animals.

But there is good news. Jesus vanquished all the dark, separating principalities on the cross. They are now on the slippery slope to destruction (Col. 2:15). If we were reconciled to God while yet his enemies, as Paul says, then it is ever so much more certain that we will live joyfully within God through Christ Jesus, since we are now reconciled to him (Rom. 5:10-11). Reconciliation is clearly taught in the Bible. And reconciliation is real, bodily and spiritual oneness with God himself (2 Cor. 5:17-20).

Not by Works

Looking back, then, at the Law of Israel, we see that sins under the Law separated Israel from God's favor only as a picture or shadow of the true separation that is inherent in createdness. Israel's disobedience and consequent alienation pointed beyond, to the outer darkness. Laws can only shake and shudder, and fling their arms wildly, pointing to the true sin of separation.

The guilt of an Israelite who broke the Mosaic Law was a shadow of the true guilt of refusing Christ. God wants to reconcile the world back to himself and become one flesh with it. But it keeps pulling away, against his will. This is why the present world is no longer good. It keeps pulling away from God. It's why even the Law itself was only temporary. All the things of this world are temporary. This world is passing away even as we speak. Death is dancing everywhere, with everyone. The floor is really crowded, with a lot of pushing and shoving. And it's real slippery. Be careful.

The Law of Israel spoke longingly about forgiveness. True forgiveness, however, was never available in the Law (Heb. 10:1-4). It was just a shadow of God's love, mercy, and grace. Forgiveness was a figure that foreshadowed the Gospel. But forgiveness of sins, shockingly, has no place in Christ, because forgiveness of sins has no existence apart from the Law. Apart from the Law sins just don't exist. It is not necessary or possible to forgive anyone for breaking a nonexistent law.

Forgiveness in the Law, like sins and righteousness and even guilt, was just an idea, just a stick drawing erased in Christ. It was just a lesson for children. God does not deal with us in relation to sin and punishment (2 Cor. 5:19). Freedom itself is what forgiveness in the Law promises eagerly. It tells of God's grace, love, and mercy. In Christ, Law has no existence, and no jurisdiction. In him, we have experienced the true forgiveness, which is freedom from law.

When the Bible speaks of forgiveness of sins, it's the same as when it speaks of washing away sins. These are metaphors. Sins are not literally washed away, or carried off, or cast into the sea. The Law was just a shadow. Forgiveness of sin is ever in relation to Law. And the Law was just a shadow. Forgiveness too, is just a shadow, a metaphor, a picture of our freedom in Christ.

Things people do, even crimes such as murder, do not separate them from God. Your past doesn't separate you from God, little one. Only your willful refusal of Christ can keep you from him. Moses was a murderer, as was King David, yet God was with them and blessed them. The apostle Paul, a murderer, found life and blessedness in Christ.

Humanity's predicament is that this temporary world is outside of and opposed to God's long-range purpose. His purpose is Christ. True salvation comes, then, by receiving Christ, not by keeping the Law. And true condemnation comes by rejecting him, not by breaking the law. Neither condemnation nor salvation are by works. Always remember that, child. Neither condemnation nor salvation arise from human works, or what is called good or bad conduct. God's will is to be gracious and merciful to those who love him and receive Christ! That's the soul of the Gospel. The Law is but a guide to show people their need to seek God's mercy, and to join in with his purpose of reconciliation (Gal. 3:23-25). The Law opens our eyes, as in Eden, to our need for transformation. We need help from outside ourselves.

Returning the Creation to God

The Mosaic Law, which represents God's will, softly whispers that good is whatever is in harmony with his will, and evil is whatever opposes it. And guess what? The very center and substance of God's eternal will is to reunite with the world, to come together again in Christ. The Law is a shadow of life in Christ. It is not itself life, but it leads to it. It leads to Christ (Gal. 3:24-25).

The very creation itself is a promise. This world was the Creator's first step toward Christ Jesus. In the beginning, God willed to separate the world from himself and call it good because it would lead to the Son. Christ is the ultimate purpose and goal of the creation. And the fullness of Christ will be oneness. God is One (Deut. 6:4). The root of the word that applies to God's oneness means to unify. His Oneness is a composite oneness, a gathering or uniting.

The initial separation of the creation from God was according to his will, and so it was good. Separation, called holiness, was part of God's original plan. It was the reason for the creation. It was what constituted his holiness. His holiness is his separation from this world. But his ultimate purpose involved reconciliation back into oneness. That's one of the meanings of the Law. Keeping of the Law symbolizes living in Christ, in oneness with God. It pictures life lived in reconciliation. This ultimate purpose was imaged earlier, in a different way, by Eve's re-uniting with Adam. As with Eve's temporary separation from Adam, the temporary separation of the world from God was originally God's will, and so it was good. It was pleasing to him.

But that separation, which was actually the creation of our world, was just the first step. His purpose now is to re-unite the world, his beloved Bride-to-be, back to himself. Just as Eve was brought back to Adam so that, together again, they could become one flesh, God is bringing the creation back to himself so that, together again, they can become one Body. The image in Adam and Eve mirrors the Creator in his relationship with the world. In Christ, God is in the process of re-constituting his Body.

Presently, since the world's separation from God is no longer his will, it is no longer good. The time for reconciliation has come. Now, the Father is pleased only in the Son. Whatever is not of Christ is no longer good. It's no longer his will. This includes all the principalities and powers, such as death, that oppose Christ. God is now calling whosoever will, to come out of this present world. He's calling us to bodily and spiritual reconciliation in the Body (Eph. 2:16; Col. 1:22). The Gospel call is a call to Christ.

The Body of God!

Jesus, of course, had a body. He was part of the earth, its noblest part ever. When he arose from death it was bodily. He left an empty tomb (Luke 24:5-6). Then, when he was received back into the

Godhead he was received bodily as well. God received a body when he received Jesus back into oneness with himself. God now has a Body again! It's a living Temple of the Spirit. And it's growing, one believer at a time, whoever who is joined to Christ.

This staggering truth is the center and focus of the Gospel and of all God's dealings with us. When Jesus entered heaven he didn't leave his body at the door. This is the very heart and mind of God, the whole message of the Bible, and the very reason and basis for existence as we know it. In this one exquisite, sublime truth we find life's supreme purpose, and the reason for our creation. God is literally receiving us to himself. United in his Spirit, we are becoming the Body of God! We share in the reconciliation of the Body with the Spirit! We have a share in the resurrection of God!

When the Father received Jesus' perfect and acceptable sacrifice, God and humanity became One. God shares in the sacrifice. God himself received Christ!

When God received Christ Jesus he received a body. Believers, being embodied, in receiving Christ receive the Spirit. In Christ, God takes on embodiedness, and humanity takes on Spirit. God and humanity come together again. We become One with each other and with God (John 15:4, 17: 11, 21-23). The true Gospel is absolutely fantastic, glorious beyond all imagination.

Jesus was fully reconciled with God when he was received into the clouds at his ascension (Acts 1:9). Those clouds symbolized the Spirit. His reception into the clouds was his entrance into the fullness of the Spirit. And with himself he reconciled all who would be joined with him by the Spirit into the one Body (Rom. 8:19-21). The Gospel of reconciliation is the Gospel of oneness.

Believers are joined to Christ by baptism in his Spirit (1 Cor. 12:13). They then become one Body and Spirit (1 Cor. 6:17). And the

Body of Christ is the Body of God! Like Jesus, believers too will be raptured into those same clouds of glory, to share forever in that same sacrosanct, divine Oneness in which God and Christ dwell (John 17:20-23; 1 Thess. 4:16-17; 2 Peter 1:4). Glory! Yes, glory!

Teachings and traditions that push the corporeity of God away in order to uphold his holiness, that slink away in fear and trembling from his embodiedness, misunderstand the very center of the Bible message, which is Christ in his fullness. His fullness will be the reunion of the Spirit and the Body of God. God is in the process of reconstituting his Body.

Into the Clouds of Glory

When Jesus was received up into the silver gilded clouds of glory, it meant that he was being received into the presence and Person of God (Acts 1:9-11). This was the completion of his baptism in the Spirit, a process which was begun earlier by the seal of the Spirit at his baptism beside Jordan's waters. His reception into the clouds meant his total immersion into the Godhead. It was total unification and complete glorification.

Like him, believers too have died with Christ in their own Spirit baptism, and are sealed unto salvation. When Jesus returns with the blessing-laden clouds of the Spirit, seated on his throne of supreme majesty, believers will be caught up into those same heavenly billows of glory (1 Thess. 4:17).

He is our Leader and Guide, the Pathfinder, and as we follow him we'll arrive at the same destination. We share his future, being fellow heirs with him. He partook fully of the same processes and circumstances that befall his brethren, except that he was first to be fully reconciled. He came into existence for the express purpose of dying, to manifest our shared destiny and to lead our way back through death's doorway into communion with God (Heb. 10:2-18). Jesus accomplished oneness with the Creator for us forever. He opened the doorway to personal, individual reconciliation and eternal fellowship with God. Because of Jesus our supremely worthy Savior, the Creator's munificence will wash over us forever in never-ending waves of goodness and glory (Eph. 2:4-7).

This is God's intent and purpose, and he will not turn from it until it is done. He will not change his mind (Num. 23:19; Ps. 15:4, 102:26-27; Isa. 43:10; Jas. 1:17). His unchanging purpose is to change his manner of existence, and receive us to himself. In this unwavering steadfastness he is the same yesterday, today, and forever. It's almost incredible. God plans to dwell with us eternally in the Body of Christ, he in us and we in him. Can there be any higher honor, or greater destiny? May his love indeed draw us into Oneness with himself. May we be made worthy.

But how? In the heart of the Gospel stands a cross. What was that all about?

Chapter THREE

The Sinner on the Cross

No Substitute Was Crucified

One of the strangest doctrines in the Bible is the idea that Jesus, although perfectly obedient and righteous according to the Law, was crucified as a sinner (Rom. 8:3; 2 Cor. 5:21; Gal. 3:13). The Bible very explicitly says that Jesus was a man without sin (John 8:46, 14:30; Heb. 2:12, 4:15; 1 Peter 2:22; 1 John 3:5). He was a lamb without blemish, the perfect and acceptable sacrifice. And yet he was crucified as a sinner. The problem arises because the cross was not mere make-believe. It was the real thing. It had to be. Everything about his death was authentic and genuine. Jesus was crucified not merely as the example of a sinner, or pretending to be one, or as a substitute for one (Rom. 6:10-11). Somehow, the perfectly innocent Jesus was made to be a sin sacrifice. Although he was innocent, actual bona fide sinfulness was crucified. Otherwise the cross was just sham and pretense. And of course, sham and pretense would have been sin.

God Was Not Satisfied

There are various theories in Christian tradition to explain how Jesus was both innocent and guilty simultaneously, but they all have unanswerable flaws. One of the most prevalent of these, with near universal acceptance, is that Jesus died as a substitute for sinners. He died in their place, as their stand-in. But every theory that depends on substitution relies on a falsehood. It doesn't answer the problem, and actually implies that Jesus was not really made sin. It keeps Jesus squeaky clean and sinless, a lamb without blemish, but in order to do this it must make the cross somehow a pretend event.

As a substitute, he was not really made to be a sinner, then. He merely looked like one. He was treated like one. The Father pretended that he was a sinner, knowing full well that he was innocent. On the cross he was a substitute sinner, a make-believe one, a pseudo-sinner. In this scenario, Jesus somehow remained sinless while pretending he was guilty, and the Father went along with the charade. Indeed, the pretense grows to the point that Jesus was every sinner, for he would take the place of all of us. Both the Father and the Son pretend an enormous lie. And that lie is enshrined at the very center of traditional Christian doctrine!

To be our substitute, acceptable to the Father, Jesus must remain sinless. Otherwise, he could not be a perfect and acceptable sacrifice, they agree. So Jesus was not really made sin, or a sinner, nor did he sin. It was all pretend, just play-acting. Substitution makes the cross event phony. But isn't phoniness a sin? Surely there must be another explanation.

When we read the accounts, we can see clearly that Jesus did not pretend. He was, through it all, conscious of his innocence. So then, the pretension must have been actually just on the part of the Father! Mercies! The tradition would accuse the Creator himself of pretense! It's a clever way of keeping Jesus innocent, but pretense, unfortunately, is never real. It's always just make-believe.

It's never true. And if it's not true, then it must be false. It has to be. Substitution would accuse the Father of actively engaging in a falsehood! Is this not very close to calling God a liar, and nigh unto blasphemy? You be the judge. Anyway, pretense definitely cannot be the truth of the cross. Salvation did not begin with a lie. Substitution can be rejected on its face. Or it can be rejected out of hand. You choose. But definitely reject it, child.

On the other hand, if Jesus had actually intended to substitute for us, then he becomes guilty of play-acting. This would put the cross on the same level as a television program, a reality show, starring Jesus of Nazareth. It would make him an actor playing the part of sinners, although he was not one. But surely Calvary was ever so much more than an interesting television show to entertain a heavenly audience. We must remember that pretense is never true. It's unreal. It's fictitious. It's false. So Jesus would have been acting out a falsehood on the cross! And God was well pleased? Mercies!

Was Jesus made sin by a phony crucifixion? No, it could not have been, because it would have placed a blemish on him and would have made his death an unacceptable sacrifice. The offering of the cross would have been refused. Jesus is not a pretender. So what is the answer?

Some theorists suggest the cross was necessary to fulfill the Law. God must be just, they say, and so he cannot overlook sin. It must be dealt with somehow. It must be punished. The cross was necessary in order to satisfy God's justice.

The problem with this theory is that Jesus' death would in fact not satisfy either the Law or God's justice. In the Mosaic Law, the soul that sinneth, not the innocent that sinneth not, shall die. Why, then, did Jesus die? If he was innocent, then his death as a sinner was unjust. And injustice can never satisfy God's Law, or justice. God is not an unjust judge, nor is the Law satisfied with injustice.

To satisfy the Law of God, the Mosaic Law, the cross absolutely must be completely just and proper, regardless of its legality or illegality under Roman law. But punishing an innocent man is neither just, nor is it the working of God's Law. Is it justice to punish the innocent so that the guilty can go free?

If you believe that, let me steal your car and your money, and you can go to jail in my place. Better yet, let them crucify you, so that I can enjoy spending your money freely and without fear. OK? That's the substitution theory, without its suit and tie, and without all the flattering words that camouflage it. It's called substitutional atonement, a doctrine held by almost all churches that call themselves Christian. But it isn't anywhere near the truth. Because substitution is always just imaginary, the theory could be called the theory of imaginary atonement. But let's call it what it is, and make traditionalists howl. Let's rip the shroud off their tradition. It's the false and blasphemous theory of atonement!

And the blasphemy gets even more vile. One popular side to this theory, told in more flattering terms of course, says that he was crucified in order to placate a vengeful, offended God who could only be turned from his intent to torture everyone by nothing less than the agonized death of his only Son. Supposedly, God's sense of justice needed to be satisfied. He needed to torture someone, anyone, preferably an innocent one, to assuage his relentless lust for vengeance.

But what kind of justice tortures an innocent man to death, an only son at that, so the guilty can go free? Is that justice? Think about it carefully. Would you torture your own child that way?

What kind of father or mother would you be? What kind of excuse could you give to the police? Will your excuse apply to God too?

Such a savage, vicious God has inspired fear and dread in countless numbers of sincere but misguided believers. They have called him a loving God only because they fear offending him. They flatter him, to get on his good side. Their God has a dark streak, but they ignore it or make excuses for it. Such a being is neither loving nor is he God. He's an idol.

Sometimes, traditionalists who hold to substitution try to excuse or soften the injustice by pointing out that Jesus went to the cross willingly, because of his great love for sinners. But willingness cannot make an undeserved death somehow just and fair. A willing injustice is still wrong. It is not fair for the innocent to suffer and die in the place of the guilty, especially in an act of pretense. It makes the Father a fake who pretends his Son deserved death in order to murder him. But no one is fooled. Well actually, most people in the churches are fooled, because they like getting away free. They're delighted to go along with the charade, for then they don't have to face the Hell-fires.

But that doesn't make it right. It compounds the crime. If the purpose of the cross was to satisfy God's sense of justice, how could a worse injustice covered with a lie accomplish that? Was not the cross the absolute epitome of injustice? Would God really be satisfied with the worst injustice of all? Crimes never produce innocence. They can't. Otherwise, our most respectable and upright people would be those in our jails and penitentiaries. Is that the case? Is that the way the Gospel works?

Another way people try to make substitution legitimate is by claiming that Jesus took away our sins on the cross. He was a scapegoat. Supposedly, the Father placed on him all our sins, and he carted them off into oblivion. But their attempt fails because sins, we remember, are just ideas. They are not tangible things. They're ideas about actions. They can't literally be placed on anyone, even on Jesus. And they can't be carried anywhere. There's no huge pile of sins somewhere in outer space, where Jesus supposedly took them all. Nor can they be washed away. The tradition takes the metaphors by which the Bible speaks of sin as if the metaphors were real. Make-believe is mistaken for reality, and falsehood is taken for truth.

Justice Was Not Served

Justice and injustice, too, are concepts that have no existence or force outside of law. Laws themselves are just ideas, remember? Moreover, to say that the Father needed his sense of justice satisfied, injects division into the heart of God. His sense of justice is pitted against his love and mercy. There is war in heaven, and it's in the heart of God! He's divided against himself. Will his kingdom stand?

And it confuses the situation. The Son, not the Father, is the one who lived and died under the Law. The Father is the eternal One who made up the Law and gave it to Israel in order to point them and all humanity to Christ. And he can just as easily erase it. And that's exactly what he did. The Law isn't a hook in God's nose.

Moreover, the opposite of sinfulness is sinlessness, not punishment. Even the most high and lofty mountains of harshest punishment can never counterbalance even one small sin. Only righteousness can counterbalance unrighteousness. Only sinlessness can counter sin. Only keeping the Law counters breaking the Law. God's Law is like Humpty-Dumpty. Once it's broken, it can never be kept by punishing someone, even if the punishment is dragged out forever, and especially if it's inflicted on the one who didn't break it. Only obedience fulfills it. This is precisely why people can never be righteous under the Law (Rom. 8:3-4). Punishment does not produce righteousness. And isn't righteousness, after all, the purpose of God's Law?

Jesus was righteous because he kept the Law, perfectly. If he had distorted the Law, dying unjustly under it, he would not have kept it perfectly. The cross would have been an act of sin, and the perfect, unblemished Lamb of God would have died in unrighteousness, an imperfect, blemished, and unacceptable sacrifice. Clearly, he didn't fulfill the Law by breaking it.

God's perfectly just Law cannot condemn an innocent man. It cannot punish the innocent so that the guilty can go free. That would be the height of injustice. You absolutely cannot achieve justice by killing the innocent, little one. You can't show that you are honest by telling lies. Injustice can never be just. It's just not possible. So, was Jesus innocent, or was he guilty? One thing is for sure. The cross was not an act of sin! But what was it?

God Did Not Abandon Him

Before we answer, we'll need to clear up a few more blasphemous but hidden implications concerning substitution and its brothers and sisters. We must not blaspheme God as some theories have done. First of all, Jesus was not crucified to satisfy the blood-lust of an angry God who was offended because two people at the edge of human history ate from a tree which he himself had planted. Second, God did not abandon Jesus at the cross, as some have said. What a horrible, profane thing to accuse God of doing!

The Father was with his Son every moment. The psalm on Jesus' agonized lips was a song of victory. Onlookers accused him of being abandoned by God. He quoted it to teach them, and us, that despite circumstances the Father had in fact not abandoned him (Ps. 22:1, 22-24). The psalm says explicitly that he wasn't abandoned. Read it. See for yourself.

God does not abandon his children. That would be traitorous and untrustworthy. It would be a violation of his word. Jesus had received the Spirit at his baptism, as a pattern for every believer who receives him (Rom. 8:11). Because of his baptism, he was God's only-begotten Son. And because we have received the same baptism, we too are God's children. Jesus' Spirit baptism is a pattern for our own. We receive the same Spirit of Christ as did Jesus. Our baptism literally joins us to him. We become one Spirit (1 Cor. 6:17). This is what makes us one with each other, and with Christ. We all share in the one Body of Christ by sharing in his one Spirit.

But if the Spirit abandoned Jesus, and he is our pattern, then God will abandon us too when we need him most! When we cry out to him he will turn his back on us. That's not salvation. It's treachery and deception. To accuse the faithful and loving Father of it is vile and contemptuous blasphemy, child. God's faithfulness is the foundation of our faith.

The Bible repeatedly tells us that God is faithful. The psalmist insisted that God would not abandon Jesus (Ps. 89:33). Standing firmly with the psalmist is the prophet Isaiah (Isa. 49:7-8). The apostle Paul nods in agreement, and insists that nothing can separate God's children from the love of God (Rom. 8:38-39). The writer of Hebrews joins them and adds that when Jesus cried out to the Father, he was heard (Heb. 5:7). Peter, filled with the Spirit, stands up with them too and, in raised voice, cries out that Jesus died in hope because God would in fact not abandon him to Hades (Acts 2:26-27). All these faithful witnesses stand together arm in arm and testify as one that the Father did not abandon the Son at the hour of his need.

But more than all these, Jesus himself asserted that God would not abandon him. His word was authoritative precisely because he was not alone (John 16:32). He told them beforehand that, when they crucified him, they would know that (1) "I am," (2) "Of myself I do nothing," (3) "I speak these things as the Father taught me," (4) "He who sent me is with me," and (5) "He did not leave me alone" (John 8:28-29). Jesus himself prophesied that his disciples would know that he was not abandoned at the cross.

Rest assured that, at the cross, the Father received the Son. His sacrifice was accepted. Jesus prayed, "Father, into your hands I entrust my Spirit" (Luke 23:46). His prayer was heard. The Father's answer was not the blasphemous, "Go to Hell, and fend for yourself! I don't want any part of you." But that is precisely what the abandonment tradition implies.

God promised to be with us, and never to leave us or forsake us (Isa. 41:10-14). He is Emmanuel. When we pass through the waters of death, he will be with us (Isa. 43:2). When we walk through the purifying baptismal fires of the Spirit, he will be there with us (Matt. 3:11). God promises to be with us forever when we receive Christ. The death of his holy ones is precious to him. And he is utterly faithful and trustworthy. He doesn't lie. Count on him completely, child.

Believers who receive Christ receive all of him, his death as well as his life (Rom. 6:6-8; 2 Tim. 2:11). We participate in the cross with Jesus. If the Father abandoned him, then he abandons us as well, each one of us. The abandonment theory would mean that, when we receive Christ, God forsakes us! Is that idea not backwards, upside down, inside out, and entirely blasphemous? Does it not drip with vileness? When we receive Christ, the Father reaches out and gathers us to himself in limitless love and compassion, forever. His faithfulness is what sustains us. Trust him. His love and compassion are real.

Increasing the Punishment

But the shroud of blasphemy against the Father does not stop with accusing him of abandonment, so we must continue pulling hard at tradition. If the truth seems brazen and rude, it's because the tradition is so vile. Gentle tugs simply will not do.

The tradition stacks blasphemy upon blasphemy. It holds that God first piled on Jesus all the sins of the world in order to aggravate and intensify his pain and punishment to the extreme! Supposedly, Jesus suffered the punishment for all the sins of everyone who would receive the lie of his substitutionary death. Not only did the Father abandon him after condemning him despite his innocence, but he also made him to experience all the multiplied, eternal suffering that all those others deserved for their crimes. And then he turned his back on him! The traditional doctrine is unbelievably, scandalously impious.

The whole idea is magical and makes no sense whatever. Eternity has no end. In the tradition, Hell is forever. How could Christ Jesus experience all the suffering that everyone who received him deserved, if that suffering was to be endless? If their sentence was to scream forever in eternal Hell-fires, and he was taking their place, he must still be there! And he will be there forever, because he's taking their place!

Oh, I forgot! It's all make-believe. God just pretends that Jesus took their place. He just pretends that Jesus is all those millions who will receive him. He just pretends that the whole thing is just and fair. He just pretends that the whole thing makes sense. Why shouldn't we follow his example, and pretend with him? Well, we could, except that we're committed to the truth. And the truth is neither magical nor nonsensical, nor pretense. Nor is the truth blasphemous.

Substitution makes friends with the childish idea that punishment somehow counterbalances sins. But, think for a moment again. When children misbehave, does a parent punish them in order to balance the scales of justice? Is that the purpose of punishment? There are no scales of justice, child! Look all you want. Search everywhere. Aim the highest-powered telescope to the skies, and you won't find those scales anywhere. And no matter how much you punish someone, that won't put Humpty-Dumpty back together. Once you break the Law, it's broken, and can't be fixed. Punishment does not make any wrong right. And clearly, clearly, punishing the wrong person for a crime is not justice! Never. Justice my eye.

Children are disciplined in order to correct them, and teach them so that they can do better in the future. But how does hopeless, eternal torture help anyone do better?

The true answer to sins and sinfulness is not punishment, but rather re-union with God. True sin is separation from God, so its answer is reconciliation with him. Jesus did not suffer in order to counterbalance an infinitude of sins on some imaginary scales somewhere in outer space, or in God. There is no need within the loving heart of the Father for eternal torture.

Jesus suffered the baptism of the cross in order to fulfill the purpose of this temporary world and to return it with himself to the Father (Matt. 3:15). His suffering, in the extreme and like no other, was his complete victory over all that this world could offer. On the cross he overcame all the principalities and powers, including death, operative in the world and in humanity. He tamed all the wild horses. And he fulfilled the Law, all of it.

Keeping the Law is what fulfills it, because it's a prophecy. It's a promise of Christ. When Christ came, he turned the promise into fulfillment. He kept the promise. The Law, given to Israel through Moses, held authority only over Israel. It was a covenant that God made with Israel, not with Americans, or Chinese, or Mexicans, or any of the other peoples. The Gentile nations have never been under the authority of the Mosaic Law, including especially the Ten Commandments. Is that shocking? Better still, is it an eye opener? Either way, we must understand that the Law is a teaching tool. It shows us God's will. His will is the fulfillment of the Law, who is Christ Jesus. The Law points to Christ like an arrow in God's bow (Gal. 3:24). In him, the Law is fulfilled. The divine promise is kept.

Re-defining Death

But let's get back to the theory of substitution. One version, or excuse, of the theory holds that Jesus' true suffering was spiritual. He suffered spiritually so that we would not die spiritually. But surprise, surprise, we're already dead spiritually. Why? It came about because Adam was told that he would die on the same day that he disobeyed. Since he did not die physically on that day, but in fact lived for almost a millennium more, it must have been a spiritual death, they say, which eventually led to his physical death. And we are his inheritors, and are dead spiritually.

But if Adam died spiritually, as they claim, how could he go on living for almost a millennium more? Was he a zombie for all that time? Are we, too, zombies, since we inherit his nature? No, death does not mean death, they explain. They've re-defined it. Death is actually separation from God, spiritually. When Adam disobeyed, his spirit was separated from God's favor. So now humans are born separated spiritually from God, having inherited Adam's nature. We're born spiritually dead.

Isn't that insane? We're dead, and yet we still live, and move, and continue to sin. Tradition has pulled a sly term-switch, and it has gone largely unnoticed. In the term-switch, not only is death separation from God, but it's also eternal. Humans supposedly possess an immortal soul or spirit. At death their body dissipates, but the soul lives forever. Some souls go to live with Jesus, while the rest go to the fires of Hell, to be tortured forever. With these two doctrines, the immortality of the soul and an eternal Hell, the term-switch is complete. Death is life. And it's eternal. Eternal death is eternal life! What a neat trick!

Hell is supposedly the place of eternal separation from God. But who sustains it in existence, then? And is not God everywhere? The truth of Scripture is that death for the wicked is destruction. It's not just a departure to another life. It's an end. It's dissipation. When the candle of the wicked goes out, it stays out. It doesn't just jump to another candelabra. And there's no one to re-light it. Death is separation of spirit from body. After death, both body and spirit dissipate. Immortality is not innate in human nature. Eternal life is only in Christ.

Death is not eternal life, child. Don't fall for the term-switch. There can be no total separation from God. We exist in him (Acts 17:28). He is everywhere (Jer. 23:24). The Spirit is active in all the creation. He sustains all things with his Word, and is reconciling all things to himself, all things (Col. 1:17-20; Heb. 1:3). He's even in Hell itself (Ps. 139:7-12). Existence isn't possible apart from God. And Hell is not forever. Nor is it a dungeon where God vents sadistic horrors upon the weak and helpless in order to satisfy his fiendish lust for justice. What kind of justice would it be to torture forever, in the most horribly unimaginable ways, simply because humans did not do things his way? Is it his way or the Hell way? God be merciful!

It was God himself, not Adam, that separated the world from himself. And it happened in the act of creation, not in Adam's apple. Adam was not the Creator. He did not separate the world, or himself, from God. And the divine creative act was not absolute separation, as we've seen. The Word of God has been the guiding influence in every age. The Bible itself is incontrovertible evidence of his presence.

Death and Disintegration

As we've seen, death is one of the principalities that govern in this present temporary creation, and work always to keep us apart from our Creator. But, being in this world and of it, death is not eternal. One bright and beautiful day the creation will be torn from death's terrible grip (Rom. 8:20-21). The world will not become a nightmare of eternal pain, but a heaven of glory, set free from its present slavery to corruption. This creation will be deconstructed, so that a new creation can be built from its remains (2 Peter 3:10-14). The powers of the heavens will be shaken, and fall. All the principalities and powers that now work against Christ, against the reconciliation that he is accomplishing, will be subdued and restrained. When the eternal arrives, it will shoo away all things temporal, including death and Hell, into oblivion. But they won't go into nothingness. They will be transformed, in the hot flames of judgment (Rev. 20:14).

At death, human bodies soon go out of existence. Bones take a little longer, but they don't change into nothingness. They are merely transformed into something new. Always, the new arises from the old. After death, the body decomposes and returns to the dust and air of which it is composed, but its elements continue in existence. Earth returns to earth, dust to dust. Only the togetherness of the body ceases, not the matter of which the body is made.

The spirit remains for a while after death as well. The spirits of those who have received reconciliation in Christ go to him to await resurrection, when they will receive their eternal, glorified bodies. They are the saints, and for them death is just a temporary separation of the spirit from the body. The spirits of those who never received Christ go to Hades, to await their judgment. At the Judgment they receive their due rewards, and are dissipated in the same flames of change in which death and Hell are thrown. Let me repeat that eternal life is only in Christ.

In death, as everyone knows, the body dissipates and loses its togetherness. The spirit, too, if not joined to Christ, dissipates and loses its identity, its discreteness and individuality. Like the body, the spirit dissolves, and goes back to God (Eccl. 12:7). The death of the spirit is the second death. It comes only to whoever is not joined to Christ (Rev. 20: 6, 14). It is not the second life. It is death, which means destruction, forever. Death is the opposite of life, not another form of it. Death is the loss of togetherness, of selfhood. Eternal life is existence in togetherness with Christ. For God and all those in oneness with him, death is just a temporary separation of spirit and body. For all others, it's the loss of individual existence.

Mortality and the Human Soul

The human soul, like the body, was meant only for this world and time. Impermanence was purposely built into the world's processes from the start. Death has always governed here with an iron hand. All the plants, animals, birds, and humans were made subject to this principle, which accomplished their impermanence. Oh, and the fish too. All things in this world have an end. This is what makes newness possible. Death makes room for new life. Death is one of the principalities that dances in the very air we breathe, and in our blood.

It goes hand in hand with change. The principle of change that works everywhere in our world allows for newness, for development and progression. It makes things move. Change is inherent in the very process of creation. And God is its foundation. He is the Creator, the prime Mover.

God planned for this world to be destroyed so that the coming new world could emerge from its passing. Planned obsolescence was put in place from the start. Humans, being a part of this world like all the other living beings, had the death principle at work in them from the beginning. Humans were purposely created impermanent, destined for destruction, in a world destined for destruction. And destruction is change. The change that humans fear most is death. And Adam was subject to it.

He did not have eternal life, or an immortal soul. Like you and I, he needed to eat from the tree of life. But he didn't. We were meant to die, child. We're children of Adam. He was mortal, a living soul (*nephesh*) like the other animals (Gen. 1:20, 24). All animals are living souls (Gen. 9:15-16; Lev. 11:46, 24:18; Acts 2:41). A living soul is merely a living creature, nothing more, nothing less. These all originated, like Adam, from the earth. The soul is the spirit that all living creatures have. It gives life. We share this spirit of life with the other animals. This breath of life comes from the great Spirit of life (Gen. 7:15, 22). The Bible shows that fish and aquatic creatures are as much living souls as are Adam, Fred, and Jeanette. Does that surprise you? If so, it's because of tradition.

The soul of a person or an animal is its life. According to God's word, animals, as well as people, are living souls (Gen. 1:20, 24, 2:7). Animals, as well as humans, have a spirit (Gen. 6:17, 7:15, 22). Animals have a soul, like humans. Surprised? Tradition has covered the truth with humanism. Shake it off, little one.

In the Bible, soul and spirit are used interchangeably. When Jesus revived a dead girl, her spirit returned (Luke 8:55). When Paul revived a dead boy, his soul returned (Acts 20:10). Likewise in the Old Testament, when Elijah revived a dead boy, his soul returned to him. And when Rachel died birthing Benjamin, her soul left her (Gen. 35:18). The two words, soul and spirit, both denote the same thing. The spirit can survive the death of the body (Matt. 10:28).

This spirit of life that every living thing possesses is a temporary expression of the very Spirit that was moving upon the face of the waters in the beginning. It's the same Spirit that inheres in the Word of creation. Because this world is temporary, its expression in living beings is temporary. Humans die in the same manner that animals die (Ps. 49:12; Eccl. 3:18-21). The human spirit, an individuation of the Spirit of life, will dissipate at the second death, unless the person has received the gift of eternity in Christ. The second death, for those outside of Christ, is the dissipation of the spirit. The spirits of all animals dissipate upon their physical death.

Death away from Christ is not another kind of life, so as to go into eternal Hell-fires. It is loss of identity, of togetherness. When the spirit dies outside of Christ, it dissipates into the ocean of Spirit from which it came. The death of the spirit is similar to the death of the body, in that both dissipate and return to whence they came. The second death of people outside of Christ, the death of the spirit, happens at the Judgment. Only those outside of Christ undergo this judgment and death.

How Jesus Was Made Sin

Well, now that we've laid the preliminary groundwork, let's see if we can answer the problem with which we started. How was Jesus made sin, while remaining innocent? In the tradition, the question is unanswerable, as we've seen. But that's because tradition is wrong on so many points.

First, we must remember that the creative act was the separation of the world from the Creator. In the beginning, the creation was temporarily separated from the Spirit. Matter and Spirit were differentiated. Next, we must remember that the Law was just prefigurative. It was just a foreshadowing of true sin and true righteousness. It was a promise. True sin is that separation from God in which the world, including humans, exists from its creation. True righteousness is oneness with Christ in the Spirit.

Finally, we saw that substitution and its corollaries could not explain how Jesus could be innocent while dying as a sinner.

Traditional Christian tradition has no answer that does not end in illogic, and too often even in blasphemy.

The truth is found in a correct understanding of the creation and of human nature. Humanity, we recall, hides the Serpent within its breast. And we recall, also, that Jesus was fully human. Jesus' words to Nicodemus help us to see how this correlates with the cross. He explained that Moses' lifting up of the serpent in the wilderness was a figure of the cross (John 3:14; Num. 21:9). Importantly, Moses lifted up a serpent, not an angel, or a dove, or a lamb. The cross was the defeat of the serpent of human nature, and the victory of Christ. The Serpent was nailed to Calvary's tree (Col. 2:15; Eph. 4:8).

With this understanding, with the shroud of tradition cast aside, we can see that, as with all other men, and like the world in general, Jesus' humanity, his creaturehood, separated him from God. He participated fully in this world. And his participation in createdness was sin, not the breaking of the Law, but rather the true sin of separation from the Spirit. He was made true sin like all men, in order to die like all men (2 Cor. 5:21). Jesus was made sin by being made of flesh, born of Mary and fully human from his conception. He was not made sin only later, on the cross. It was from the beginning, from Mary's womb. We recall that Mary offered a sin offering for both of them (Lev. 12:6; Luke 2:22-24).

True sin is separation from God, pictured in the Law as breaking a commandment. Jesus did not break any of them. With respect to the Law he was sinless. His very humanity, as is the case with every human, was what separated him from the Creator. That separation was the true sinfulness in which the whole world languishes. Shockingly, then, he died for his own sake as well as for that of the people (Rom. 6:10-11; Heb. 5:3, 7:27, 9:7). Contrary to the tradition of substitutionary atonement, he did not die merely for the sins of others, in an act of pretense. His own humanity required reconciliation.

He had undergone a partial reconciliation at his baptism, when he received sonship and the seal of the Spirit. His ministry that followed was accomplished in the power of the Spirit. Later, at his ascension, the enfolding clouds welcomed him back into the inviolate and sacrosanct being of God. His total immersion into the Spirit completely erased the true sin of separation. Jesus died so that he could be divested of his mere humanity and be transformed and exalted into the divine inner sanctum. He died for himself as well as for others (Heb. 5:3, 7:27).

But this was not as their substitute. The cross was not a drama in which Jesus was magically made to be sin. Nor was it a stage for Jesus to pretend in utter pain to be sinful while the Father went along with the deceit, and left before the show was over. Jesus died in order to lead sinners separated from God like himself back to God. With respect to the Law, he was innocent, an acceptable sacrifice. With respect to the world, he participated fully in its separation from God.

At his baptism he was reconciled with God, but he still retained his human nature and body until the cross. He died in order to get rid of the serpent completely. The serpent was nailed to the cross. Jesus died as a lamb without blemish, and was received bodily into the Godhead after his resurrection.

The cross did not involve substitution or pretense. It was real, in all its pain and gore, and sheer unmitigated horror.

Jesus Needed Reconciliation

It is shocking and difficult for traditionalists, of course, to accept the fact that Jesus, the perfect, unblemished Lamb of God, was crucified as a real sinner. Nevertheless, this is the clear teaching of Scripture. Christian tradition has taught, wrongly, that God only made him appear to be sinful, or to take the place of sinners. But that idea throws the mud of dishonesty all over God. He becomes an unrighteous judge with muck all over his face and innocent blood on his hands, a pretender perpetrating a tremendous deceit. Inanely, the tradition tries to keep God and Christ Jesus innocent by heaping bucketfuls of sinfulness upon them!

When Jesus received the Spirit, he and God were rejoined into oneness. But, it was merely the seal of the Spirit, not the full immersion to come in his exaltation. And like all other humans, even those who are baptized in the Spirit like him, he too still needed to die, in order to divest himself of the leftover sinful nature (Eph. 4:22-24; Col. 3:9-11). He was human. That's what humans do. They die. Everybody does it.

Like other humans who receive Christ and are sealed by the Spirit, the man Jesus still needed to be fully clothed with the divine nature (Zech. 3:3-7). As yet he had only the seal of the Spirit. So he died, that is, his Spirit was temporarily separated from his body for three days. His death was temporary, a three-day separation. Then the Spirit returned, and reentered his body. But it was a body in the process of being transformed into the eternal Body of glory. Mary did not recognize him.

His new body, like the original creation, did not arise from nothingness, but rather from the transformation of his old body. That's what creation is, a change. And Jesus is the beginning of the new creation of God. When he arose, it was as the firstfruits of a plenteous harvest of followers who would arise like him. Like his followers, he needed to be transformed. Flesh and blood can't inherit the kingdom of God (1 Cor. 15:50). He died in order to be transformed and enter into glory (Heb. 12:2). He repeats the divine archetype. And he's the pattern for us. We will definitely follow. Did he not say we would?

No Immaculate Conception

In their humanity, both Jesus and his mother Mary were alienated from God. When Jesus was born, Mary was required to offer a sacrifice for both their sin (Luke 2:22-24). According to the Law, she was unclean for seven days, then she underwent purification for another thirty-three days (Lev. 12:2-8). After this, to remove her guilt, she needed the priest to offer for her a sacrifice. The sacrifice, of course, being under the Law, was powerless (Heb. 10:1-4). It was just a picture of the coming offering of Jesus. In obeying this law, Mary showed that she was a sinner like everyone else, and needed the reconciling sacrifice of the Lamb. And she offered the prescribed sacrifice not for herself alone, but rather for both herself and her son!

As we saw, sin isn't just the actions that humans perform in unrighteousness. It isn't the breaking of Israel's law. Humans do not comply with the Mosaic Law because of self-centeredness, the outgrowth of our humanity. Mary, partaking of creaturehood, was sinful by her very nature, and passed this nature on to Jesus, from mother to son. The doctrine of immaculate conception sees sin as only the breaking of the Law. Sin runs deeper than the

Law, and than the Church's understanding. Or should I say her misunderstanding? Yes, I said it. And I meant it.

Crucified With Christ

Many of the muddy currents of error that swirl around the cross in Christian tradition spring from a faulty interpretation of the Old Testament sacrifices. They are thought to be substitutional, and this same idea is carried over to the cross. But substitution is not the basic meaning of the Old Testament sacrifices. The entire sacrificial system in Israel was a series of pictures. To understand it, we must see it for what it is. In a pictorial, prefigurative way, it was a promise that God and humanity would be joined as one.

The Law was a covenant between God and Israel that united them in a unique relationship. He was their God and they were his people. This relationship pictured God's greater, ultimate purpose, which is true togetherness with his true people. The sacrifices of Israel were foreshadowings.

The Law, including the rules of sacrifice, preached the Gospel, beforehand. It prophesied of Christ. The whole Bible is his story. And as we are joined with him, it becomes our story too. The Bible is the story of the saints, as well as of Christ. It's the story of the creation's reconciliation with the Creator, the fantastic tale of God and the world, separated in the beginning, coming joyfully together again in the fullness of Christ.

Reconciliation is foundational to the entire history and intent of God's dealings with humanity. It defines God's will, and constitutes salvation. It tells of God's great love for his Bride. It's the essence of the Gospel message, the purpose of the creation, and the reason of our existence. It goes beyond eternal life, giving the reason for it and its destiny. Jesus lived and died to reconcile us to God, in his Body (Eph. 2:14-16). In Christ, God and the world are drawn together again. And that's exactly what sacrifice pictured. It foreshadowed reconciliation.

The root idea, the *sin qua non* in reconciliation is reunion. Any interpretation of the magnificent saving work of Christ that misunderstands or rejects this basic, indispensable principle is necessarily false. Any doctrine that contradicts the unity between God and Christ in his followers is anathema, contrary to God's will and word, and satanic. That sounds harsh, but the point bears emphasis. Keeping us separate and apart from Christ is what Satan does. He's the great Opposer, ever pulling the world away from God. One of his favorite methods is to employ false doctrines and blasphemous traditions. And one of his favorite places to do his dirt is in church.

It doesn't matter if a doctrine is popular. It makes no difference whether a belief is traditional. Neither popularity nor tradition create truth. The truth is found in the word of God and is consistent with reality, for reality itself is the expression of truth. And truth expresses reality. It doesn't matter how many priests or religious leaders teach a false doctrine. It can never be made true by pretending, or by majority vote, or persecution, or even by shouting from behind a pulpit. What matters, is if it's consistent with the word of God, and with reality.

So, we need to be perfectly and absolutely clear in regard to the sacrifice of Christ. Let's consider it more closely. We'll see more clearly why the doctrine of substitutional atonement, so central to Christian tradition, is false, and why the sacrifices in the Old Testament do not support the tradition.

The Problem With Substitution

Jesus partook of creaturehood like every human. And creaturehood entails death. Surprisingly, perhaps shockingly, the Bible teaches that he died for his own sin, as well as for the sins of others. He died to sin in the same manner that we die to sin (Rom. 6:10-11). Jesus our high priest needed to offer for himself as well as for the people (Heb. 5:3). His sacrifice is not repeated, but it was for himself as well as for them (Heb. 7:27). That's difficult to receive, isn't it? The churches have kept the crowds contented with the candy-coated errors of tradition. But the truth is, that in his humanity Jesus was separated from God. He needed to take steps to undo that separation.

He needed, first, to receive the Spirit. This happened at his baptism. Then, like every other human who receives Christ, he needed to divest himself of the leftover human nature. He needed to die. And, in dying for himself, Jesus could not logically substitute for himself. He didn't die as his own substitute, a nonsensical idea. Jesus did not inanely switch places with himself on the cross. He was not a substitute. But he was a perfect sacrifice, and the ideal pattern for all others. Being the pattern, the cross gives the meaning of all the Old Testament sacrifices.

A popular passage that substitutionists like to quote is found in the book of Isaiah (Isa. 53:4-6). On first reading, the passage appears to be substitutional, but only through the shroud of tradition. If we remove the shroud and read it with a clear and receptive mind, we can see that the passage speaks of mutual participation, not substitution (Isa. 53:11-12). It says that he made many righteous by his knowledge, and interceded for them. He was a teacher and an intercessor, then, not a substitute.

And this is not merely our speculative opinion. The disciple Matthew, taught personally by Jesus himself and inspired by the Spirit, interprets the same passage in Isaiah to mean that Jesus bore away our sicknesses and evil spirits (Matt. 8:16-17). Bearing away is not substitution, child. Let me repeat. Matthew says explicitly that Jesus bore away sins, not that he pretended to take them on, vicariously. John, Paul, and the writer of Hebrews concur (John 1:29; Rom. 11:27; Heb. 10:4, 11-12; 1 John 3:5). Moses does, too. According to Moses, God himself explained the sin sacrifice as taking away sin, not as substitution (Lev. 10:17).

Can it be any clearer? Jesus did not become sick when he healed the sick. He did not become demon-possessed when he cast out demons, or on the cross. God's word says that he bore away our infirmities by healing them, not by substituting for us. Substitution would contradict Matthew and all these other faithful witnesses. It would contradict God himself!

The sin offering in the Law, foreshadowing the cross, was meant to bear away sins and to make atonement, that is, to produce reconciliation between the offerer and God (Lev. 10:17). Its meaning, while still only figurative in the Old Testament, was oneness between the offerer, the victim, and God.

The worshipper would eat part of the sacrifice. Eating means to assimilate, to take to oneself that which is eaten. So, eating of the sacrifice symbolized oneness of the offerer with the victim. And part of the sacrificial victim was offered up in smoke. It symbolized that God himself was sharing in the meal (Lev. 3:11, 16, 21:22, 22:25). Sacrifice pictured both the worshipper and God coming together in the sacrificial victim.

The sacrifices pointed away from themselves to Christ Jesus, our true sin offering, in which both God and humanity come together. This is why we partake of the Lord's Supper. In symbol, we eat his body and drink his blood (John 6:56). The symbolism means that we join with him in his sacrifice and in his life. It signifies that we are one Body in Christ. And Christ is God. We are reconciled to God and to one another in Christ.

The apostle Peter interprets the passage in Isaiah similarly. He says that Jesus bore our sins to the cross so that we would die, not so that we would not die (1 Peter 2:24). The apostle Paul interprets the cross in this same manner (Rom. 8:3; 2 Cor. 5:14-15). If one died for the sake of all, he says, then all died. It was not substitutional, for they died too. It was exemplary and inclusive. Substitution would mean that they didn't die, because he died in their place. That's not what the verse says.

The writer of Hebrews agrees with us, and disagrees with the tradition. He writes that Jesus bore away the sins of many (Heb. 9:28). When the Bible says that Jesus died to take away our sins, it means that he takes them away as we participate in him. That's important. He bears away our sins only as and when we become one with him. Otherwise, the unconverted and unbelieving would be saved without coming to Christ. That's not the Gospel, child. It's nonsense.

Much of the confusion comes because the tradition treats sins as if they were tangible objects, to be literally borne, or washed away, etc. The tradition treats metaphors as if they were real, and takes no account of the figurative nature of sins. Sins under the Law, we recall, are just shadows of true sin. What the sacrifices signified was that, when we partake of Christ, we are changed into a condition acceptable to God. He then receives us into oneness with himself, erasing the true sin of separation. The object or goal of sacrifice, of course, was to be accepted. Acceptance says it all.

When the Bible says that he died for our sins, it means that he died in order to deal with them and help us (2 Cor. 5:15). When it says that he died "for" us, it means that he died on our behalf, in our service, to our favor, in order to make all its benefits available to us. It does not mean that he died in our place as a substitute.

If Jesus had died as our substitute, we would not need to die. But he calls us to die with him. His suffering and death were not to prevent us from suffering and dying. If that were the purpose of the cross, obviously it would have failed miserably. Followers of Christ continue to suffer and die, do they not?

And substitution is always fraudulent. Take this truth to mind, little one, and burn it into your memory. Substitution is always fraudulent. The substitute is always only imagined to be the one for whom substitution is made. It is only pretended. It is always false then. The substitute is never the one for whom substitution is made. Substitution foolishly pretends that one thing is another, or that one person is another. The doctrine of substitution makes the cross counterfeit! It calls Jesus a pretender and a liar, and calls God a divine fraud who devised the whole scheme. Rather than honor Jesus as a selfless hero, it literally drips with blasphemy.

The sacrificial victim's death was representative and symbolic. The animal offered in sacrifice represented the person who offered the animal. In symbol, the offerer became one with the victim, by eating of the sacrifice. The animal was not a substitute, then, for the offerer ate of it, in symbol becoming one with it. And astoundingly, God himself symbolically ate of the sacrifice. It meant oneness between offerer, the victim, and God. The main idea was oneness.

Now think carefully, child. Because God ate from the sacrifice, substitution would mean that the sacrificial victim was substituting not just for the offerer, but for God! And a substitute for God is an idol. Substitution would make the sacrificial victim an idol! It would mean that Israel's sacrificial system was a system of idolatry, then, commanded by God himself. Isn't that insanely blasphemous? Supposedly, God was in symbol offering himself to himself, in order to forgive himself? That's twaddle.

Sacrifice pictured the worshipper joining in the cross. It pictured the death of the worshipper, and union with Christ and with God. Its goal was to gain God's acceptance. Sacrifices preached beforehand the Gospel of reconciliation. That's what we've said all along. The cross was the means of reconciliation. That's what the sin sacrifices of the Old Testament prefigured.

Jesus said that those who would come after him must deny self, take up their own cross, and follow. Does that sound like substitution? To truly follow, then, we would have to substitute ourselves for the whole world! That's ridiculous. And he never said "Just follow me for a little while, because you can't follow all the way." He calls us to follow him because it's possible to follow him. It's a reachable goal, not a carrot on a stick.

On the cross, Jesus offered himself, not a lamb, or a substitute for himself. And he is the perfect fulfillment of that which the sin offerings in the Law prefigured. If the Law had pictured substitution, Jesus would have offered a substitute for himself, because he was fulfilling the Law. And he was not only the victim, but also the offerer. He offered himself, as our perfect example. He, too, needed reconciliation. And every follower is with him on that same altar (Rom. 6:5-6; Gal. 2:20, 5:24). Jesus' death meant the same for him as it does for his followers (Rom. 6:10-11). Like him, we offer ourselves, to be joined with him.

If Jesus had died as our substitute, it would not be necessary any longer that we offer ourselves, or that we die. But true sin is not the breaking of the Law, remember? The only thing that can fix the problem of a sinful nature separated from God is the transformation of that nature, and its reunion with God into oneness. And, that's precisely what Christ Jesus accomplished. He reconciled us to God. He is not reconciled as our stand-in, however. That would mean that he did not reconcile us! It would actually negate the cross. A substitute Savior is no savior at all.

The Cross Was Not a Payoff

Neither should we suppose that his death was a literal payment of any kind. Only re-uniting eliminates separation. If you lose your arms only re-attaching them can make you whole. Punishing someone will not give you your arms back. Giving someone else two arms in your place and then pretending it's you will not help you. Giving you money can never make things right. And what if you should lose your head? Would punishing someone fix you? Would money help? Payment for sin is just a metaphor, and should not be taken literally.

The cross is not a business transaction. God does not need to be paid off in order to look the other way. He cannot be bribed. The idea of real payment speaks the unthinkable, that God would accept, nay, require the life of his own Son as hush money to cover up the crimes of others! But life is not money, nor does God need any. Nor does he barter or trade money for mercy. The death of Jesus was not an indulgence!

Sin Is Not Our Fault

Substitution misconstrues the nature of sin. We must remind ourselves that true sin is not what we do or fail to do in relation to the Law, which was just a set of ideas, remember? Sin is what we are. We're not to blame for what we are, for having been created. It wasn't our choice. God himself created us this way, the first step in a larger process. The creation cannot be faulted for being created. Nor can humans, along with the other animals, be faulted for being the animals that they are.

Why then does God find fault? He doesn't! That's the whole point of the Gospel. It's the very essence of the story of the creation and salvation! The truth of the Gospel is freedom from law and sin. It's the joyful shout of God's grace, and the epicenter of his loving will. The Law, and all the other principalities and powers of this world, lose their steely hold on us when we receive Christ. Reconciled with God, we have overcome death and all the unrelenting principles of impermanence that govern in this world. In Christ we have triumphed over them all. We've become champions, dear one.

He doesn't condemn us for being a part of this world. He offers salvation to any who will come freely to him and be reconciled. Whosoever will, may come joyfully to the fountain of living waters and drink deeply of life and liberty. Reconciliation is the very reason for the creation, and the purpose for humanity. It's the point of it all. Death isn't a punishment. It's a limitation, like the inability to fly, or to breathe under water, or walk through walls. Would you walk through walls? Come to Christ. Would you live forever? Come and be reconciled to God.

He doesn't fault anyone or condemn anyone (John 3:17). The Law condemns. But God is not under the Law. And he invites us to join him in his divine freedom. Christ has bridged the sinfulness of separation. In him, the world is reconciled to God, transferred from the dark dominion of death, into the resplendent kingdom of light and love (Col. 1:13).

No Equality in the World

But, does God owe salvation to those who never heard of Christ? No, the world doesn't revolve around humanity. And neither is life a business deal. Humans have done nothing to earn eternal life. Why should he save anyone? Salvation is by God's grace, not by his debt. The Creator is not the Debtor. He is free to do with his own as he pleases (Rom. 9:19-23). It was never God's will to receive everyone indiscriminately into himself. Nor was it his will to receive all the other animals.

When we blame God for not saving everyone, or for the misfortunes of life, we misconstrue his purposes, and rebel against his sovereignty. It's the subtle idolatry of humanism. Rather than blame God, as if he owes humanity and is guilty for not treating everyone alike, we should busy ourselves in sharing God's true word of salvation with everyone who will listen. In receiving the word, they can receive the living Word.

God is not unfair or evil for not saving everyone. We mustn't forget that good is the will of God, not that which is beneficial to humans. If he chooses not to save everyone, it's his prerogative. Our notions of fairness are derived from law, based on justice, and do not bind him. He is not bound by the humanist idea, based on law, that everyone should have a chance, and preferably an equal chance, at salvation. He is not bound by legalism or humanism.

A gardener who picks flowers, or weeds her garden, is not thereby unjust and evil. And when she pulls weeds, she is not accused of being unfair. Why, she may even spray for bugs! She is not required to treat all her plants equally. After all, it is her own garden. And if humans are free to care for their gardens, is God not free to tend to his own?

Even under the law, equality is not justice. Contrary to what we are taught in school, and sometimes in church, there is no equality in this world. It's impossible. And God does not treat us all equally. If there were equality, it would be grossly unfair and inappropriate. Jesus didn't teach it. The idea doesn't come from the Bible. It comes from the Preamble to the U.S. Constitution. And it's impossible, anyway.

We're all unique. We're special. None of us are exactly alike. Absolutely nothing in this world is exactly like something else. We may see certain similarities, but comparing apples to apples is just as invalid as comparing apples and oranges. No two apples are ever alike even if they seem to have similarities. Unlike things can never be equal, ever. That would be like saying that two equals six. If you believe that, let me trade you this new one-dollar bill for your old hundred-dollar bill! OK?

Would it be just and fair to make everyone wear the same size shoes? Would it be right to make everyone eat the same kind of food, in equal amounts? Jesus wants us to love one another, not to treat each other exactly the same. Love is a special manner of living that makes others special. Equality is a falsehood that treats everyone the same, and calls it fairness. Thankfully, God deals with us in special ways. He gives us differing talents and opportunities (Matt. 25:15-28). He has made each one of us unique and special. And some are more special than others.

But he doesn't owe anyone salvation. He saves those who receive Christ. That's his choice, and his prerogative. It's his plan and he's sticking to it. The decision was made even before the creation. This is his world, and he calls the shots. Indeed, it's his own Body. He has chosen to save all who will join in his eternal purposes (1 Tim. 2:4; Titus 2:11; 2 Peter. 3:9). And his eternal purpose is, you guessed it, Christ.

Joined With Christ

God is merciful and gracious. His grace is not marred if he doesn't save everyone. It is to his matchless glory that he saves any of us at all! Nevertheless, his grace is available to whoever will receive him. This is why we must preach the true Gospel of the true and living God of mercy and reconciliation, rather than the vicious and vengeful God of law, pretense, punishment, and abandonment. He is the God of truth, not the trickster who makes the cross into a sleight-of-hand called substitution. Does it make sense for churches to preach a sadistic God of deception, substitution, and eternal torture, while making excuses for him by insisting that he must be just, that he must be bound by the rope of law? Is law binding even on God? Is he not stronger than Samson? I think you know the answer.

Even thieves, drunkards, and murderers can be forgiven in Christ, because true sin is separation from God in our createdness. So, true forgiveness and salvation are free, found in union with Christ, and not dependent on keeping the Law. They're found in union with Christ. He's not our substitute. He's our leader and guide. When the Spirit joins us to him we become part of the Body of Christ. Because we are One, his death becomes ours, and our death becomes his. We are crucified together with him (Rom. 6:6-11). We share in the cross! We share in Christ's sufferings.

This all occurs because we are joined to him. When we receive him, we are united with him in death, resurrection, and eternal life. If he died as our substitute, he would also live as our substitute. He would live in our place! Do you really want a substitute to live for you, to take your place and live eternally for you? Will you call that salvation?

Neither was he baptized in our place. Nor can we be baptized in one another's place. Substitution is always a sham, an act of pretense, as if one thing were another. We can't eat the Lord's Supper by proxy. Nor can we have faith by proxy. We can't receive Christ for one another. We can't be saved by substitution. Each of us must receive Christ individually, personally. The atonement is participatory, not substitutionary. And this included Jesus himself.

If you were hungry, would it help if I were to eat a delicious, nutritious meal for you? Why not? Well, it's likewise with salvation. Substitution doesn't work, and Jesus didn't do it.

The cross was not an inane comedy. We must each one personally receive Christ, be baptized in the Spirit, and partake in the Lord's Supper for ourselves, each one individually. We must each one of us partake in the cross, not just pretend ludicrously that Jesus is participating in it in our place.

In the Law, the sacrificial animal represented the offerer, remember? In symbol, the worshipper offered himself on the altar in the hope of being accepted. A pleasing sacrifice was a picture of being received by God. This is what happens when we receive Christ, our acceptable sacrifice. When we receive him, we are joined with him on the altar. And God receives us to himself!

Participation, Not Imitation

Just think. When we receive Christ, God receives us. Doesn't that make you want to jump and shout? This is why Jesus invites his disciples to follow him, not just to cheer him on from the sidelines and flatter him. A substitutionary atonement denies Jesus' call to follow. It invites disobedience and disregard of his call to be crucified with him. It makes discipleship a mere imitation of Christ, which even Satan can do, and does. It makes copycat Christians, rather than true followers. His call is to walk in the Spirit, child.

True discipleship is real. It doesn't just pretend to follow Christ or to be crucified with him. It's genuine, actual participation with him, in oneness, together. Imitation is what Satan does, remember? He pretends to be like God. He puts on an act and tries to mimic Christ. But there is nothing worthwhile in his actions. Mimicry becomes mockery. To pretend Christ-likeness is actually to imitate Satan, little one.

Christ is not a pretender. Nor does he want you or me to become one. Pretense is falsehood. Don't do it. Don't pretend Jesus suffered and died in your place so that you don't have to die. And don't accuse Christ Jesus of doing it. That's blasphemous. An imitation diamond is pretty much worthless. Imitation gold is fool's gold. And an imitation Christ is an antichrist.

We must be joined to Christ, and he must live in us. Only then will we be like Christ. Only then will we carry within us the image of God. Always, union with Christ is vital. We participate in his death, and he in ours. Like Paul, we are crucified with him, in order to live with him and in him. The truth is ever and always participation, not pretense. We're players, not spectators.

We must get in the game, not just sit in the stands and eat hotdogs and popcorn.

If Jesus does not truly reconcile us with God, if he only reconciles himself as our substitute or stand-in, is he not then keeping us separated from God? That's Satan's work, people! Substitution means that instead of bringing us into oneness and communion with God, Jesus has entered into communion himself with God, inanely pretending that we are him. It means that he has not reconciled us. He has come between God and us. That's the very definition of an idol! By promoting substitutional atonement the tradition has been busily doing Satan's work! The Bible tells us that Jesus is our mediator, not our substitute (1 Tim. 2:5; Heb. 8:6). We must not allow anything, including Christian tradition, to come between us and the truth. Christ Jesus is a bridge, not a wall of separation.

In Death As In Life

If we are joined to him in his death as in his life, then, because he died, we too have died (Col. 3:1-3). And because he lives eternally, we too shall live eternally. And that eternal life will be in an embodied manner. Matter and Spirit are not totally incompatible. This present creation, the world of matter, then, has never been totally irreconcilable with or completely separate from its Creator. God's holiness does not mean wholly other, as some would say, and some have said. This world, which in the process of time included humanity, in some sense was with God and was God in the beginning. It's true that the Word became flesh in uniting with the man Jesus, but even before that, the Word had been instrumental in forming our world. The world was separated from God and transformed as he spoke it into existence. The world is the expression of God.

The notion that God is wholly other contradicts the scriptural view of creation to its very face, and denies the work of Christ. The world issued from God, from his very substance (John 1:1-3; Rom. 11:36; 1 Cor. 8:6, 11:12; Col. 1:16; Heb. 2:10). The name, Emmanuel, means that God is ever with us. He has always been here. That is the Gospel message. The world originated from God and will return to him in Christ, in loving reunion. And it will be embodied. Body and Spirit will come together again. God's Body will be reconstituted.

Staying Together

God is deep, unfathomable love. Such love desires closeness and togetherness. Love means hugs and kisses, not aloofness and distance. Love works toward reconciliation when there is separation. The idea, then, that God is so holy and exalted that he is absolutely and forever separate and distinct from the creation, and from us sinners, misunderstands his nature and detracts from the truth of his great love. He wants us close. He desires togetherness. We cannot demonstrate our love, or honor him, by keeping our distance. You don't hug someone by pushing them away.

Sometimes, or many times, even religion gets in the way of his love. This is true of the mainline churches of Christianity, large or small, liberal or conservative. Well-meaning worship can become a subtle kind of idolatry. Praise can become flattery. It may appear ever so pious and worshipful to praise God and elevate him high and above the vagaries of this world. But when such praise or doctrine separates the worshipper from God it is neither true worship nor sound doctrine. Worship in such a case has become specious and evil. It has become satanic. Worship and praise can be satanic? Yes, child, worship can be satanic, if it pulls people away from the true God of true love, with actions or with words. True love brings togetherness. It brings oneness. Satan separates.

Praise in the Old Testament was merely a picture, a figure, a chalk drawing pointing beyond itself. Like the other things of the Law, as it was practiced in the Old Testament it was both figurative and temporary (Col. 2:22). It was worship of God at a distance. It was just a shadow of true worship, not its essence. True worship is service, not a service. It is not a program flattering God, thinking to honor him by pushing him away, even if the push is upward. True worship is a life of ministry to Christ, in Christ. The fulfillment of the Old Testament figure of worship is to walk in the Spirit, doing his will. True worship is to live life in glad and grateful oneness with the Savior.

He desires more than closeness. If we reject his invitation to communion and togetherness under the guise of elevating him beyond reach and away from ourselves, we are in effect pushing him away. Even keeping him at arms length denies his great love. It's true that Enoch walked with God. But he wants us even closer. He wants us to walk in him, and he in us (John 17:21-23). It's why we must receive Christ. Putting any distance between ourselves and God rejects the clear desire and intent of the Creator. And it denies the work of Christ, who has reconciled us with God and has brought us together in the warm and intimate fellowship of his love.

True worship wells up from a heart of gratitude, and is accomplished in the Spirit. It draws us to God in thankfulness, wonder, and joy. He is our God, we are his people, and we are one! We are One! The songs that we sing, and the prayers that we offer, should celebrate and deepen our oneness with him. They must be offered in that oneness, that is, in the Spirit. If not offered in the Spirit, they are offered in the flesh, and deny his love even while they appear to proclaim and manifest it.

Humility, too, can go awry. Sometimes, instead of pushing God up and away through misguided praise, people withdraw themselves from him by false humility. They may appear to be immensely pious as they "humble themselves in the sight of God," but that's just Old Testament shadow. When humility becomes a means to distance themselves from him it becomes evil. It's Satan at work again, hiding under the shroud, slyly and steadily pulling the worshipper away from God.

True humility denies self and runs to God's goodness trustingly, as a child to a loving Father. It declares gratefully that he is the Creator of our salvation because of his great lovingkindness and everlasting power and dominion. It draws us to him. True humility does not run from God. It's an updraft of the Spirit that wafts us up into the very heart of our Creator.

Neither praise nor humility should separate us from our loving Father. Any doctrine or tradition or practice that opposes the true reconciliation and oneness that is his will is part of the satanic system of this world. Whatever separates us from God is idolatrous and evil, wherever it is found, yes, even if it's found in churches that claim to worship the true God.

How It Really Happens

In order to understand how the reconciliation works, we must come out from the darkness of myth and magic. The truth of the cross is not make-believe or metaphor, both of which would in fact deny the reconciliation. Make-believe only pretends that something has occurred, when in fact it has not. Metaphor says that something akin to reconciliation has taken place. It, too, denies real reunion.

It's not enough to pretend we're reconciled, or that we have a relationship with God similar to reconciliation. Pretense has no place in an open and true relationship, or in proper worship. Reconciliation is actual union with God. Union with God is real, as real as the One who reconciles us. Unlike Adam and Eve, we must not fear to approach God, for we have been clothed with Christ. We do not stand spiritually naked before the throne of grace. As we come before that august tribunal, we are clothed with Christ. And Christ is God! So we have God himself returning the creation to its Creator, the Spirit within us merged in total harmony with the Spirit who sits on the judgment seat. And he will be well-pleased.

Participants, Not Spectators

The Word that erupted out into the primeval beginnings as God spoke will not return to him without accomplishing his purposes. But it will surely return (Isa. 55:10-11). This occurs in Christ, who was joined bodily with God at the Jordan as a seal and figure of his later death-baptism and resurrection into the gilded clouds of glory (Acts 1:9). Through death, Jesus was received back into the fullness of the divine nature and given the name above all names (Zech. 3:3-; John 17:5; Phil. 2:8-9; Heb. 1:4, 2:9). He is the great Número Uno. We too, joined with him, are received with him into the heavenly glory, into the divine Oneness (John 17:5, 22).

It cannot be over-emphasized that believers are baptized with the same baptism that Jesus underwent (Rom. 6:3-11). He did not substitute for us. We must come like him to Jordan's cold waters. The heavens must open above us too, and we must be sealed like him by the Spirit, joined with him to await our own resurrection and exaltation at his return. Meanwhile, we bear the cross with him (1 Cor. 12:13-14).

Our baptism in the Spirit is our death with Christ, just as the offering of a sacrificial lamb pictured death with him on the altar. To receive Christ in his fullness means to accept death with him, as well as life. We must receive all of him. The agony comes before the ecstasy. The thorns come with the rose. Baptism involves our own cross. Jesus was not baptized so that we would not have to be baptized. His cross does not exempt us. His death does not keep us from dying. When we receive his Spirit, we receive his cross too. We die with him. We are joined with him in life, death, and ultimate, all-conquering victory.

We, too, will share in the absolute authority of Christ Jesus. Jesus' exaltation, as was his life, is the pattern for every saint (Phil. 2:8-9; Heb. 2:9-17). We are participants, not spectators. Joined in the Spirit, we too can say, like Jesus, that we are sent from God and are not of this world (John 15:18-19, 17:18-19; 1 John 4:4-6). And for this, the world will ridicule us. But that's okay. They ridiculed Jesus too. He is the pattern for every saint. Nor was he ridiculed so that we would not be.

We belong to the new world that God intended even before the creation. We have been saved from temporality, delivered from death. As believers we have freely opted to join in the eternal purposes of God and to do his will. We have cast ourselves trustingly into his outreaching arms, and have been made One with the Spirit. Indwelt by the Spirit, we are being carried by the swift, unstoppable current of history that is flowing uphill back to its Source! This river of life will flow until the final day, and will empty its waters into the unfathomable ocean of God's benevolent will. Its abundant waters will carry us on into eternity. This is the future of every saint.

Dying As a Sinner

Jesus' death was the one sacrifice in which all who are joined to him share. Being one with Christ, his death is ours, and our death is his. Importantly, our death then has the same meaning as Christ's death (1 Cor. 15:50). And, since our death is for the purpose of crucifying the old sinful, carnal nature, we know that the death of Christ Jesus had this very same meaning (Rom. 6:6). He died as a sinner, as one of us. Yes, he died for us, that is, for our benefit, on our behalf, but he also died for himself. Jesus, too, required metamorphosis. His humanity needed to be transformed and glorified.

Although he was sinless in reference to the Law, Jesus died as a real sinner, not as an imitation of a sinner, or as a mere picture of a sinner. The cross was not a sham. What Jesus did at Calvary is real. He totally vanquished all the power of the Serpent, both within and without. His sinlessness was his complete obedience to the will and law of God. He fulfilled it all. In that respect, he was unsullied. But sin is more than the breaking of a command, and righteousness is more than keeping a command. It runs much deeper.

Sin is within the nature of humanity itself (Rom. 8:6-11; Eph. 2:3). Our carnal nature is temporal, and must be put off, in order to put on the glorified, eternal nature of Christ (1 Cor. 15:42-56; Phil. 3:21). Even when there was no Law people died (Rom. 4:15, 5:13-14). Jesus died too, even though he fulfilled all the Law perfectly. The principalities and powers in the world that pull away from God are inside of us, as well as in the world. Satan is a squatter within our own heart. We are serpents, a generation of vipers (Rom. 8:6-11; Eph. 2:3). We need a changed nature. We need metamorphosis. We need to be like Jesus. Yes, we need help. But God knew this would be the case even before he created. It's all in his divine plan.

On the cross Jesus died unto sin, as do all who receive death with him (Rom. 6:10). Jesus died in sin, as a human whose very humanity was estranged from God. His humanity was lifted up and hung on the cross like the serpent that Moses lifted up in the wilderness (John 3:14; Rom. 6:10, 8:3; Heb. 4:15; 1 Peter 2:22). The serpent is a symbol of the separating principle, especially in humanity, and including especially the humanity of Jesus. That's shocking, isn't it? But its truth comes from the lips of Jesus himself. As Moses lifted up the serpent in the wilderness, the Son of Man was lifted up on a hill called Calvary.

Slaying the Serpent

The serpent symbolizes the basic, natural antagonism of the creation toward its Creator. This tendency or principle of antagonism toward God in humans is called Satan. He is the Opposer, who works against God's desire for reconciliation. The world, including the world of humanity, lying in the power of the wicked one, is oriented toward self-service and survival, away from the original togetherness that once existed. The principalities of this world, the laws of nature working with Satan, were placed in the world in the original act of creation with the purpose of separating the world from its Creator. That's their job, and they're still working at it, like a herd of wild horses, skittish and unbroken, always running from God.

The original pull of separation from God that was placed within the world from the beginning was originally good, being God's will. But now it has become evil, since God now desires reconciliation. Here is the answer to that age-old question about the origin of evil. The principalities and powers that still pull the world away from God are now working against his will (Eph. 6:12; Col. 1:16, 2:15). They have not changed. This is why Satan, the principle that pulls away from God, has now become the Opposer. He has fallen from favor. He fell not in the dark, misty ages before the creation, but with the coming of Christ (Rev. 12:7-11). Christ Jesus cast him out of his place in heaven (John 12:31-32; Col. 2:14-15).

The serpent principle, the natural drive to self-fulfillment and self-service, has enabled the various species of living things, including Homo sapiens, to survive. He was in Eden, talking to Eve within her own mind, tempting her to satisfy her thoughts and desires (Eze. 28:13). He was not a snake, nor was he a spirit using ventriloquism through a snake. Snakes don't talk, child. Humans do. And why would God curse the snake, indeed the whole genus of snakes, if a spirit were the real culprit? The serpent in Eden was Eve herself, her own selfhood, her human nature (Jas. 1:14f, 3:15). Even before she disobeyed, her orientation was inward. It was a desire to fulfill her desires. The serpent still speaks to humans in the same way. He speaks to our heart and then, many times, from our lips.

However, this spirit or tendency was not sinful at first. In the beginning, it was God's will to separate the world from himself, Body differentiating from Spirit. Originally, the world's tendency away from God was good. Satan was not evil at first, for he was doing God's will. He was not yet the Opposer. He was, indeed, the principle or power, or highest angel, that God used in the creative act of separating the world from himself.

Nevertheless, separation was only the first step in God's marvelous plan. God intended to reconcile the creation back to himself. Satan, being the natural tendency in the world to separate from God, to run wildly away, is now out of harmony with God's will. He is no longer good.

He fell to evil from his exalted position of goodness, importantly, not in the long ages before the creation, nor in Eden, but at the cross. He was cast out of heaven through the ministry of Jesus (Luke 10:17-18; Rev. 12:7-11). He fell when Adam fell. Their destiny was intertwined. God foretold that both would die together (cf. Gen. 2:14, 17-19). Satan's fall did not happen in Eden, or in the nameless ages before the creation. It began beside the Jordan, at Jesus' baptism. And it's still going on today, all around us. Whenever a person receives Christ there's a muffled thud. Can you hear it? It's Satan falling.

Satan showed his face with that first law in Eden. The law took his mask off. It opened the primal couple's eyes. It revealed the natural human orientation inward toward self. Adam would die because of his innate enmity toward God's long-term will. Left to itself, human nature ever does its own will rather than God's will. So the Law, even in Eden, spoke of the cross and of Har-Magedon, where Adam will surely die (Rev. 16:16, 20:10). And with his death the serpent inside him will die.

In order to accomplish reconciliation, Jesus needed to fully overcome this spirit of selfishness and antagonism toward God. He needed to confront all the principalities in the world and within his own flesh. Every vestige of this inward-looking, natural human tendency to survive, to continue itself and exist apart from God, needed to be subdued. Adam was told to take dominion over the earth. Christ Jesus, the greater Adam, fulfilled this word too. Thank you, Jesus.

His pain and suffering were total, in order to subdue the Serpent totally, completely, to the utmost. Jesus' humanity, like that of every other human, fought savagely to survive, to come down from the cross and live. The Serpent mustered against him all the concentrated horror, shame, and sheer agony of which a human is capable, in order to prevent Jesus' willing death on the cross. The cross was the Serpent's last-ditch stand. He mustered every power and device at his disposal. It was the whole, desperate world of darkness gathered against Christ Jesus.

But heroically, magnificently, our great Champion conquered the Serpent and died, willingly. The cross became the turning point of history. Incredibly, astoundingly, on the cross Jesus withstood the full force of the entire creation's runaway alienation from the Creator. On the cross our Savior stepped in front of the whole breakaway world, bore the full brunt of its gathered inertia, and stopped it in its course! Then he turned it on its axis and sent it spinning like a ball back toward its Creator! He changed the direction of the world. What a matchless, magnificent Champion!

And he's our leader! Jesus died to fulfill this world's temporariness, and to usher in the new world of eternity. He did it all. Alone and single-handedly, he stopped the whole stampeding world in its tracks, turned it around, and is now herding it back to the Creator, whistling and singing, rounding up the strays. He wore Adam's crown of thorns and turned it into the pure gold of the victor's crown (Gen. 3:17-19; Heb. 2:9). His victory was complete. What a Savior!

A Bodily Return to God

Through the cross, Jesus offered his humanity to God, an acceptable sacrifice without blemish (Heb. 10:5). Forty days later at his ascension into the clouds of the Spirit, God fully received him back to himself (John 17:5; Acts 1:9). This was the culmination of Jesus' acceptable sacrifice and baptism. All believers participate in this same sacrifice and baptism, and will be received like him by the Creator into the sublime Oneness (Heb. 9:28, 10:10).

And because Jesus was of the earth, having a physical body, his reception back into the Godhead happened bodily too. It was not just a return in the Spirit. The tomb is empty. In his Body, resurrected and glorified, he reconciles to God all who are joined with him into the one Body (Rom.8:19-20).

They too are reconciled to God in the same way in which Jesus was reconciled, to share his life, his glory, and his sovereignty. And they will share in the divine Body of God. When they receive the Spirit, as Jesus did at his baptism, they are sealed unto the Savior. Then, upon their bodily death and resurrection, they will be received into the same clouds of the Spirit that received Jesus (1 Thess. 4:17). They too will be exalted into the divine glory, to await the Resurrection. This is the heritage of every saint! It's glorious beyond description.

The reconciliation is not just a return to personal favor with God, as the tradition would have it. No individual humans were with God in the beginning before the creation, not even Jesus. Reconciliation must deal with the entire creation's return, then, not just with individuals. Think of the world as a yo-yo, or maybe a boomerang. Anyway, you get the picture. It's a return, and it's real.

Reconciliation is a genuine, bona fide return. And a real return requires separation first. You can't return if you've never left. To be reconciled to God, a person must have at one time been separated from God after having been together with him. The Gospel of reconciliation thus hints of an original oneness between the Spirit and the world. Reconciliation is, then, a physical and spiritual rejoining of that original togetherness which was separated by the act of creation. Creation was the differentiation between matter and spirit. Nothing else has separated the whole creation from God. Sin didn't do it, as we've seen. The fact of reconciliation is strong evidence, then, that the creation was at one time within God. The false doctrine of *creatio ex nihilo* would deny the original oneness, and true reconciliation. It would deny the Gospel. But if we deny the Gospel, what's left?

Sinless Now and Forever

Yes, Jesus died as a sinner, for himself as well as for others. But now, having died and risen, Jesus is without sin, for he has been fully reconciled back to God, no longer separated in his humanity (Heb. 7:26; 1 John 3:5). In his humanity he was tempted like all men, but committed no lawlessness (Heb. 4:15; 1 Peter 2:22). He was not separated from God by breaking the Law, for he fulfilled it perfectly. Jesus was separated from God by his creatureliness. Like all the race, his humanity itself was sin. So he nailed that serpent to the cross. And he's our great and perfect example. And an example is made to be followed. Does it mean we too have a cross to bear? Yes, child, it does.

Our sins, things we do or don't do because of our humanity, do not separate us from God. Our nature itself separates us from him.

Our participation in the creation, with its built-in alienation from God, is what constitutes true sinfulness (Gal. 3:22). Sins are but expressions of our nature, of our innate sinfulness which cannot subject itself to God's Law (Rom. 8:7).

So the answer to sin is not through works. Trying harder to be holy doesn't help. It hurts. The answer is to try less. It's impossible to acquire sinlessness by human works. That would be like trying to change into an angel by pasting wings on your back and jumping off your roof. It won't help you to fly. Don't try it, child. Humans can't change into angels, or birds, or anything else. Humans are humans. And that's not a compliment.

If you're human, face it. Look yourself in the mirror, and tell yourself that you can't change yourself into a sinless person. Give up trying. Then, give yourself to the One who can change you. Invite the Spirit into your being. Don't rely on works. Don't rely on your actions. Your actions are the Serpent's handiwork. The things of the Law cannot reconcile us to God, even if we could keep it. The leopard can't change his spots. The full, proper answer to the human predicament is reconciliation by reception of the Spirit. We must be reborn, of God. Our bodies must become temples of his Spirit, houses of worship, serviceable to his will.

The Spirit works through the Word of God. As we receive the Word, who is Christ, the Spirit of life enters and unites with us. This is the baptism of the Spirit (John 6:63; Jas. 1:18). Like Jesus, we are begotten from above and become incarnations of his Word (1 Peter 1:23). The Word becomes flesh once more in a marvelous way in every true believer, as it did in Jesus at the Jordan.

In receiving God's Word, we join in the long-range plan of the ages. Like Jesus, we become the incarnation of Christ. As we walk in him, as we willingly allow the Spirit to fill us and control us, our bodies become temples. Our lives become living sacrifices offered to God in worshipful service, and accepted into the Oneness that is the goal of every sacrifice. This is the reason of our existence, and the outworking of our salvation. In him, we have a good and meaningful reason for living.

The true Gospel does not involve receiving Christ and then trying to follow the Ten Commandments, or any other laws. That's the error of judaizing the Gospel, of trying to make it an extension of Judaism. It's a trap into which many Christians have fallen (Gal. 3:1-14). The truth is that we must receive Christ and then follow him personally, directly, heeding his inner voice. We must walk in the Spirit. To serve Christ we must serve Christ. Doesn't that make sense? To try and serve him through an intermediary is to commit idolatry!

But if we refuse Christ, who is the Word of God made available to us, and the divine purpose for our creation, then we refuse the very reason for our being. We will miss our opportunity to be included in God's project of reconciliation, and life everlasting. To refuse Christ is to refuse glorious oneness with God (John 17:21-23). Eternal life in and with our Creator is the reason why we are saved from death and transformed into a new creation. To reject Christ then is the very height of stupidity and folly. Tragic beyond words, it will bring eternal death in the Hell-fires. Scary, huh?

Chapter FOUR

Truths and Falsehoods about Hell

A Question of Reality

The doctrine of Hell is perhaps the scariest and ugliest doctrine in Christian tradition, conjuring up unspeakable terrors in the imaginations of those who take it seriously. It has been one of the favorite themes of churchmen to frighten people into acceptable behavior. But it has also helped people face the precariousness of their mortality, and through the years has been the means of bringing countless people to Christ and salvation.

Yet, despite its historical position in the mainstream of Christian doctrine, some sincere believers today question the reality of Hell. It seems foreign to the nature of a loving God who is gracious and merciful, and ready to forgive all our sins. How can a loving God condemn anyone to an eternity of torture? Why would he create such a place? The doctrine is difficult to maintain side by side with the Gospel of grace and mercy. The two ideas seem so contradictory.

One answer has been that Hell was made for Satan and his angels. But that doesn't solve the dilemma. Even if it was made for them, and not for us, is it not just as horrible? Is God's loving nature exonerated because he didn't originally intend eternal torture for humans, but only for the Devil and his angels? And if it was only for angels, why does he send humans there? What of his foreknowledge? Didn't he know all this evil would happen, and he did it anyway, knowing the vast majority of humans would have to be sent there? It doesn't make sense.

Another answer transfers the responsibility from God onto the one who refuses to accept Christ. In effect, the individual who refuses Christ and the Gospel chooses eternal torture, they say. But that is not true. Refusing Christ is not the same as choosing to be tortured forever. The result of a choice should not be confused with choosing the result. They're two different things. If I choose to drive too fast and then I have an accident, this is not proof that I chose to have an accident.

Moreover, not everyone has been given the Gospel. What of those countless numbers who never heard about Christ and salvation? Will they indeed be tortured forever because they refused Christ? Or worse, will they be tortured forever because Adam ate an apple? Hell is the result of Adam's apple?

Because of these and other questions and concerns, for many people Hell just can't be real. It doesn't fit with a God of love and mercy, or of justice. And if this doctrine is questionable, what of other central Christian doctrines? Birds of a feather flock together. If this individual is unsavory, might his friends be just as bad, or worse? Should we let them in? Nevertheless, the Bible does seem to present the reality of a place called Hell. Is it real? Or, have we misunderstood? Is the tradition right, or wrong?

While the idea of Hell may give a brisker step to those who accept its reality, others find it unbelievable. It makes Christianity appear not just unloving, but also quite unreasonable. The doctrine should be clarified so that, if it is not scriptural, it can be thrown out. If it is scriptural and real, it needs to be held up and taught widely so that people might order their lives in accordance with its reality and truth.

The Traditional Nightmare

Perhaps, before continuing, we should clarify what we mean by the traditional doctrine of Hell. In the tradition, it's a place of eternal punishment for sin, for the things people have done against God. It's a place where God sends the wicked who remain outside of Christ, to spend eternity suffering pain similar to being burned alive. They have no hope, and no end to their torment. It hurts God enormously to send anyone there, but those who are sent there deserve their punishment, even if we don't understand it, for God is just. He would not send anyone there who did not deserve such a destiny.

But it's hard to imagine anyone so wicked, any crime so heinous, as to merit an eternity of total, unlimited pain. Hell is forever. How could an eternity of pain be the proper, reasonable, and just punishment for even a long lifetime of sins? Take a scale, child, and put a human lifetime on one side, and eternity on the other. Which weighs more? Or take a ruler, and measure them. Which is longer? The punishment is infinitely out of proportion to the severity of the crime, isn't it? And it is pointless. It serves no useful purpose such as rehabilitation. All it does is satisfy God. He must be just. Oh?

Is it possible for humans to act outside of their own nature? Can they do anything at all that they can't do? No, humans can only do what humans can do. And God made them the way they are. Will he then torture them forever for doing what he made them capable of doing? It makes no sense.

When this idea is coupled with the idea that God is omniscient, that he knows everything and knew in advance that people would be sinners, the whole notion inevitably calls the goodness of God very seriously into question. After all, he created the world. He created the angels too. Didn't he know they would rebel? Didn't he know that his highest, loveliest, and most cunning angel would turn out to be such a fiend? Whose fault is it, finally?

He created the animals and birds too, and the fish. Don't animals rob from one another, and kill and eat one another? Don't whales eat krill? Who made the animals? And why is humanity singled out for Hell, while the other animals go free? Because the doctrine seems so illogical and so unbelievably monstrous, and so inconsistent with the character of Jesus, it would not find any credence whatsoever, except that the teaching seems to arise from the Bible itself. Indeed, the proponents of the traditional doctrine of Hell point out that Jesus spoke more about Hell than did any of the other prophets. This, supposedly, proves its reality. And it does, for what Jesus spoke is the truth. We can safely trust in the reality of what the Bible calls Hell.

It's Real, But Is It Right?

So, perhaps we should revise our question. Instead of asking whether or not Hell is real, let's ask whether the traditional interpretation is correct. Perhaps Hell, although real, is not the raging bull that tradition keeps in its corral to frighten children and their parents. Maybe the tradition is the result of failure to understand what the Bible actually says about it. Do you think that's possible? Can so many Bible interpreters be wrong? Can the majority have gone astray?

The answer, of course, must come from the pages of the Bible, from which the doctrine has purportedly been taken, and where the truth can be found. Traditionalists quickly run to the Bible when the doctrine is challenged, so let's follow them there. The truth will be logical, and harmonious with God's eternal plans, and especially with his character and nature as revealed in Christ. Does it pass muster? We'll see.

The Illogic of It

At first glance, the traditional doctrine of a place of eternal torture for breaking the Law of God just doesn't seem to fit in with the picture of a loving God. Hell does not seem loving at all, does it? And it appears the same even at second glance, or third glance. It just seems awful and frightening, and most people try to put it out of mind and ignore it. As we approach it here, it barks at us as if to scare us away, so that we don't get too close. But we must not be frightened away. The fence of logic will hold. We won't be bitten so long as we stay on the side of truth. So let's look at the doctrine closely, being sure that we stay on the side of logic and reason, and truth. We must stay true to the Bible.

Punishment Is Not Legal Tender

Proponents of Hell sometimes maintain that it's God's answer to the problem of sin. Supposedly, sin is the cause of this world's fallenness, the ground from which has grown all the pain, suffering, and death that is woven into the fabric of our lives. Hell's fires are the answer to sin, they say. Sin calls for punishment.

Supposedly, it somehow balances or pays for the wrongs that sin has accomplished.

But, as we have already seen, the scales of justice are just a metaphor, a figure of speech someone invented. They have no real existence. And anyway, the true counterbalance to sin is not punishment, but righteousness. And punishment can never change sinfulness into righteousness. Only the cross can do that. In the tradition, Hell's dwellers will never be made righteous.

Torture does not counter or repair sin, even if it is dragged out to infinity. Infinite torture is in fact infinitely worse than the sins it is supposed to correct, but doesn't. Infinite torture would be infinitely evil. If all the multiplied pain and suffering in the world is evil, how can inflicting infinitely more pain and suffering be good, even if God does it? And if Hell is good, why do Jesus and all the churches work so hard to keep people from going there? Would God multiply evil forever, and call it good? Is God guilty of eternal sin? You know the answer.

If disobedience is the problem, then obedience, not punishment, should be the answer. But the fires of Hell cannot turn disobedience magically into obedience. If they could, that would eventually do away with the need for Hell, since the wicked would eventually be made righteous. And it would make Hell a means of salvation! Is Hell really the answer to sin? Is Hell a kind of Savior? After all, if disobedience causes death, should not the answer cause life? Is Hell the source of eternal life? No, child, Hell does not answer any of the above. It has no redemptive purpose, and is not the answer for sin. The answer for sin is the cross. The churches have blasphemously substituted Hell for the cross!

Nor can punishment pay for sins, as if sin incurred a literal debt. Payment for sin is just another figure of speech, not to be confused with reality. Sin isn't a tangible commodity to be bought and sold on the stock market. Sins are just ideas about noncompliance with other ideas called laws. And punishment is not money or legal tender either. Hell just doesn't make sense. And truth, as we have seen, must make sense.

The Limits of Law

The Law's claws can't fasten on the saints. They're already dead, having died in Christ (Col. 3:3). The Law was the ministry of death (2 Cor. 3:6-9). Once death has occurred, the Law loses its hold. When death occurs, the Law is satisfied and no longer has jurisdiction (Rom. 6:7, 7:2, 6). Death of the lawbreaker, not eternal torture, satisfies the Law.

And the Law was just a shadow anyway, a figure fulfilled in Christ. Abiding by the Law was a foreshadowing of abiding in Christ. When Christ fulfilled the Law he erased it. It disappeared. It was a prophecy, a promise. A promise kept disappears with its keeping. A prophecy fulfilled is no longer prophetic. It loses itself in its own fulfillment. Jesus kept the promise of the Law, and changed it into fulfillment. And where there is no Law, no one can be justly punished to satisfy it. Being only temporary, and meant for this world only, the Law cannot reach through the iron bars of its cage into eternity. It cannot exceed its jurisdiction. Its long arms cannot reach past death. God's children are safe from its grasping, steely clutches.

For those outside of Christ, both Jews and Gentiles, Law's limit is death as well. The wages for sin is death, which means destruction, not eternal life in agony (Rom. 6:23). Christ has abolished the Law of Moses. He nailed it to the cross. But don't take that literally, because laws are just ideas, child. That's just a poetic way of saying that he did away with the Law through the cross. The Law will cease to exist, even for those who keep it in mind, with their death and consequent destruction. Obviously, the Law can't punish where it has no existence. Nonexistent Law cannot exercise jurisdiction in a Hell that doesn't exist, over people who don't exist.

Out of Proportion

In any event, an eternity of torture is not in harmony with the Law. In the Law, punishment was in proportion to the crime. It required an eye for an eye, a tooth for a tooth. It was never a head for a toenail, or a thousand eyes for one eye, or a trillion teeth for one tooth. It was balanced and just. An eternity of pain would be out of all proportion to a few short moments, or even a lifetime, of sin. It would make the Law unjust. That's a self-contradiction, an oxymoron. The Law cannot be unjust, or transgress itself. Take a scale, child, and put a tooth or an eye on one side and, well, you get the point.

The Wrong Answer

Because punishment doesn't answer or correct sin, moreover, it's an altogether illogical and inappropriate answer for it. If lack of righteousness in the present is the problem, will punishment in the future solve it? Punishment is useful to correct future behavior. In the Law, it was a figure of the consequences of failing to be reconciled to God in Christ. But when there is no chance to influence anyone's behavior, no chance to draw sinners to reconciliation in Christ, punishment has no useful function.

An eternal Hell would defeat God's sovereign will and purpose of lovingly reconciling all things to himself. Only a corrupt medieval Church that catered to the aristocracy could have thought such a state of affairs was proper. In their ideal society the elite, uncaring and thoroughly decadent few dance away the days and nights, feasting on the delicacies of heaven, while the vast multitudes of commoners suffer unimaginable cruelties. It makes God into a monster who keeps a dungeon beneath his castle to torture his captives forever and ever.

Is God a House Divided?

Love is eternal (1 Cor. 13:8). Even faith, and the hope of eternal life, will cease. Death, too, will come to its end. No, justice is not eternal either. Justice and injustice are but functions of the Law, mere drawings on a chalkboard. But there's no chalkboard in heaven. Law has no jurisdiction over its Giver! Its cold, merciless claws cannot tighten around the loving heart of God. His supposed legalism cannot be pitted or counterpoised against his love. He is not caught between the proverbial rock and a hard place. Nor does he suffer from an unresolved inner conflict between his love and a never-fulfilled sense of justice. He does not bear a grudge forever. He's not divided against himself. God doesn't punch his own nose to spite his face. Nor does he keep an eternal punching bag hanging in the closet. He just doesn't.

Questions of the Soul

All that is in the world is temporary. Humans drink from the muddy puddles of impermanence until they come to the clear living waters of eternity. Until they drink from the Spirit they are merely intelligent, morally aware living creatures. Well, somewhat intelligent. But they have no eternal life and no immortal soul. At death, their body dissipates. After the Last Judgment, their spirit will dissipate in the second death as well. Only God is immortal (1 Tim. 1:17, 6:16). Yes, only God is immortal. Remember that, child. To live eternally, humans must receive Christ. Humans without Christ do not live forever, separated from God in a place called Hell. That idea is totally absurd. Eternal life is only in Christ.

Immortality is a reward, a prize, a gift that is bestowed upon whomever God chooses. It is not and never was inherent in humanity (Rom. 2:7; Eph. 2:3; 2 Tim. 1:10). Humans are living beings in the same manner that the other animals are living beings. We all share the same breath of life (Gen. 6:17, 7:15, 22, 9:10-16). If the human spirit is immortal, then the spirit of animals is immortal as well, for we all share the same spirit of life. So then, what happens to animal souls? Is there a Hell for animals too? Is there a heaven? No. Well then, perhaps they're in Limbo?

If humans had an immortal soul, from where would it originate? Is there a spiritual holding tank somewhere, filled with souls waiting to be born? Do they line up wherever humans copulate, pushing and shoving, fighting to see which one gets to enter the new fetus? Remember, God is no longer working on this creation. It is finished and the Sabbath has come. He's not creating any new souls. So, from where would the newborn souls come? And what would happen to any unborn souls? Must we copulate so that more souls can escape their invisible prison? The whole thing is absolute twaddle.

The childish notion of an immortal, indestructible individual human soul doesn't make sense, and it's not scriptural. The Bible does not teach it. And without this immortal spirit, the doctrine of Hell as a place of eternal, conscious torture has no footing, and falls into the bottomless pit of its own falsehood. It is not scriptural, and should be discarded. If we would truly follow Jesus and do God's will, we must walk upon the solid ground of truth. Watch your step, there.

The Truth of It

The true Bible teaching is that the world originated from God, at his command. His Word is the causative agent of creation. It's what makes things become what they are. His Word, or Logos, is the agent that initiated the original differentiation between Body and Spirit. Every individual spirit and body is the handiwork of the Word. Nothing was created without him (John 1:3). This means, then, that the Word is everywhere. And the Spirit and the Word are One. There exists, then, an ocean of Spirit engulfing all the creation. God's presence is in all things (Jer. 23:24). The world exists in him (Acts 17:28). This Spirit that's in all things becomes individuated in every human, and indeed in every living thing, in conjunction with their physical individuation. As they take form, the spirit does also.

As the earth individuates, as it takes on form and becomes a person through the natural processes of procreation and growth, the Spirit individuates with it. Just like human and other animal bodies originate from the earth, the human spirit, like all the others, originates from this ocean of Spirit immanent in all things.

The spirits of humans are individuated units of Spirit that take form from the great Ocean that engulfs the world. They have originated from God. They are eternal and immortal, then, for they are individuations of the Spirit. But their individual identity is not eternal, just as physical individuals are not eternal. As the physical decomposes at death, so also does the spiritual. Death is the end of each individual's togetherness, the dissipation of a person's individuality.

An ice cube exists only when you freeze water in the form of a cube. Water takes the shape of its container. If you put the ice cube on the table and it melts, the cube form ceases to exist, even though the water remains. The human spirit is like water poured into human form. It holds this form for a while, for so long as the physical form exists, but in the hot flames of death it melts and goes back to God.

Now then, does it make sense for God to separate units of himself into spirits, and then torture them eternally? Is God some sort of masochist who punches his own nose never-endingly to appease his insatiable sense of justice? The traditionalist answer is yes. The traditionalist answer is blasphemous.

Different Forms of the Spirit

The Bible says that the wicked will be destroyed like the other animals (2 Peter 2:12). Sheol will consume them all (Psa. 49:14, 19-20). At death, both men and beasts all go to the same place (Eccl. 3:18-21). And it isn't heaven. They all share the same breath or spirit. At death, the flesh returns to the earth, and the spirit returns to God (Eccl. 12:7). As they do, they lose their individual form, like raindrops that fall on the ocean. Death is not a separation from the Creator, but rather from oneself. The soul says goodbye to

Fred, and Kelly, and Frieda, not to God. This is true for both unsaved humans and the other animals.

Adam's sin did not separate him from God, because the Creator is everywhere (Ps. 139:7-12; Jer. 23:24). As we noted, God continued to speak with Adam even after his sin. It was his humanity, rather than sin, that separated him from God. But the separation is not absolute. We live and move and exist in him (Acts 17:28). For Hell to exist, it would have to exist in God. The doctrine of an eternal Hell looks like blasphemy to me. Smells like it too. Don't swallow it, child. Spit it out.

Nothing can exist totally separated from God. Absolute separation from him would be nonexistence. If Hell is total separation from God, it cannot exist. Death does not mean the nonexistence of the spirit. It means its disintegration, its diffusion. The ice cube melts, and the cube form disappears. Likewise, when a person dies his form goes out of existence and the spirit goes back to its original state. It goes back to God. We're speaking here, of course, of the wicked.

As we have seen earlier, sin is a figure in the Law, and is temporary. Sin is erased by the annulment of the Law, which Jesus accomplished. It is not erased by torture. This present creation will be dismantled in order to construct the new creation in Christ. Christ and God are One. Whatever does not serve God in the new creation in Christ will be destroyed. Satan and his servants will be no more. The creation's primeval separation will have been healed in the reconciliation that Christ is accomplishing. Law is not a part of Christ, nor is punishment. A place of eternal punishment would wrongly make the Law eternal, and place it in Christ. The Law has been annulled. And it was only for Jews anyway, not for Gentiles. There is no dungeon under the New Jerusalem.

An eternal Hell would mean that God and the creation will never be completely reconciled. God will remain dead forever! He will have no Resurrection! Well, maybe he won't be completely dead. He'll have a deformed Body, though, just a shadow of his former self, a lame, crippled, cancerous God unable to heal himself. Is the doctrine not blasphemous?

A False Start

Other childish and mythical, even magical, assumptions in Christian tradition are likewise based on a failure to understand God's word. For example, the doctrine of eternal torture often goes hand in hand with original moral perfection. Adam and Eve, and all the animals, were supposedly created in a problem-free paradise where all was harmony and mutual goodwill. An original utopia sounds wonderful, but the Bible doesn't teach this childish fantasy.

Supposedly, when Adam and Eve disobeyed they fell from their state of perfection and immortality, somehow magically carrying the whole creation down with them. In this fantasy, even the farthest stars were affected. Nature itself changed. Storms gathered in the skies. Thorns grew on the rosebushes. Animals began eating one another. Adam and Eve were kicked out of their idyllic, edenic home, and now they had to work for a living. Somehow, although they had died spiritually, they gave birth to children who were living souls themselves. But tragically, their children bore the fallen nature of their parents. This all happened when they ate some fruit from a tree. Oh, and they had to start wearing clothes!

Strangely, although God is omniscient, Satan out-maneuvered him. He was able to thwart God's original plan by inducing this first human pair to disobey. God had to initiate plan B. Now Christ must come and die horribly, because God must have revenge. The Serpent had shattered God's perfect world, and God must now try to gather up some of the pieces. He must put Humpty-Dumpty back together, somehow. But he can't, or won't, so he must torture forever.

Compared with the numberless multitudes that will perish, only a sparse remnant will be saved. The Devil will have spoiled most of God's best handiwork. The creation has been ruined, and humanity, God's crowning work, has been corrupted. But the loving God will have revenge. He will destroy this world and build a new paradise to replace the first one that Satan ruined. Then he will horribly torture these humans, every hapless little child of Adam who had the misfortune of being born, along with the Devil and his angels. And he'll call this hideous, hellish horror justice. Of course, God knew in advance that all of this would happen, but he did it anyway. Huh? What?

Such a mythical, unscriptural scenario is make-believe and magic, a childish fantasy that belongs with Santa Claus, the tooth fairy and, pardon me, the booger man. Christians must grow up and put away these childish myths. No, Virginia, there really is no Santa Claus. The false doctrine of the Fall vilifies God and glorifies Satan. Let it go, child. Throw it into the trash bin along with the tradition of endless torture in Hell. And leave it there. Better yet, take it out to the curb for the junkman.

The First Days

What really happened back there? The Bible doesn't divulge the length of the first days. It doesn't look at its watch and announce they were twenty-four-hour periods. Clocks, hours, and minutes did not yet exist. A day was one period of darkness and light, period. God called the period of light day and the period of darkness night (Gen. 1:1-5). How long were they?

It doesn't say. Presumably, ordinary days were like today, repetitive and regular. But the days of creation are not ordinary. They are long periods of creation, consisting of darkness followed by daylight. Adam was told that he would die on the day that he ate of the forbidden fruit, and yet he lived almost a century of years more! The six days of creation were not twenty-four-hour intervals, then. They were long periods, made up of an untold number of ordinary days.

The light of creation was not light in the abstract. The first light was the light of the sun. When the earth was formed, the sun existed already. But there was a mantle of ice that enveloped the earth and cloaked it in dense vapors and darkness. In time, the vapors cooled, letting the light through, allowing the sun and stars to be seen. Still later, the disturbance that melted the ice and caused the flood cleared up the atmosphere, and the seasons began.

We saw earlier that Adam could not have died only spiritually. A living body with a dead spirit is, again, magic. Adam wasn't a zombie! He wasn't the star in a horror movie, an original Frankenstein. If he had died spiritually, if his spirit were dead, how could he pass on a living spirit, an immortal soul, to his children? Was Adam a dead man walking (Jas. 2:26)? No, dead men don't walk, and neither do they produce children that have living souls. It just doesn't happen, except in monster movies, and in the morbid imaginations of churchmen. Yes, new definitions of death can be invented, but as we saw, they all end up in error and blasphemy, and must be rejected.

Did Adam fall from close and intimate fellowship with God? Is that the death that he died? That fantasy is not found in the Bible record either. In the tradition, the supposed lost fellowship between God and Adam was from the beginning an arms-length one. It was just an easy cordiality and friendliness. Adam and Eve were never in oneness with God. They were close to him, on speaking terms, but closeness is not oneness. The supposed fall must have dropped them even further away from God. Does this mean that, now, God had to yell at them? Was God's "Where are you?" to Adam an indication that he didn't know? It makes no sense. The Bible says God continued talking with them as before.

Nor does the biblical account say that Adam died because he ate the forbidden fruit. Eve wasn't Snow White, and the fruit wasn't a poisoned apple. Adam died because he was chased away from the tree of life (Gen. 3:22).

The various and sundry dogmas and doctrines that deal with the beginnings of the human relationship with God that Christian tradition has invented, have no true scriptural support. Nor can they support the doctrine of eternal Hell-fires. They're neither scriptural, sensible, or moral. They dishonor God. Eternal torture is not the answer to Adam's sin or any other. The traditional doctrine of Hell should itself be thrown to the fires. What does the Bible really say about the death of the wicked?

Destruction of the Wicked

It says that whoever sows to the flesh reaps corruption (Gal. 6:8). God will destroy the wicked (1 Cor. 3:17). Their end is destruction (Phil. 3:19). Sheol will consume them (Ps. 49:14). They will vanish like smoke (Ps. 37:2, 9-10, 20). They will be as if they had never existed (Ob. 16). The wicked dead will not live forever, either in body or in spirit (Isa. 26:14). The Bible repeatedly shows that the wicked will be destroyed. Surely no one believes destruction is eternal life. Or do they? Yes, oddly, most Christians do.

Death, too, like everything in this present creation, will be destroyed. Death will die. Death means decomposition and destruction (2 Cor. 5:1). Destruction does not mean separation from God as tradition would have it (1 Cor. 15:26; Isa. 25:7-8; Rev. 21:4). Death means separation of spirit from body, but not from God. For the saints it's just a temporary disjunction of spirit from body. It's not destruction, and it's not eternal. We must not allow traditionalists to play the game of termswitch on us. This present wicked world will be destroyed, not just separated from God (2 Peter 3:6-7). It's already separated from him. God destroyed Sodom and Gomorrah as an example of the End-time destruction (2 Peter 2:6). If you want to know what that's like, open your Bible and read what happened to them. The opposite of life is death. The opposite of salvation is destruction. End of story.

Fires of Judgment

Proof is everywhere. Death of the body brings its decomposition. When a body dies, it rots (Acts 2:26-27). It oxidizes, either fast, resulting in visible flames, or slowly, resulting in the flameless heat of putrefaction. In either case, fast or slow, the oxidation that occurs in death is the same chemical event. At death everyone burns, whether in the searing flames of cremation, or in the flameless decomposition of putrescence.

John the Baptist prophesied that Jesus would baptize with the Holy Spirit and fire (Matt. 3:11). Baptism of fire is figurative, symbolizing immersion into the purifying Spirit of holiness that burns up all ungodliness, that is, all separation. For believers, Spirit baptism is immersion into Christ in the holy fire of the altar. Their sinfulness is burned away, leaving only the purity of Christ that withstands the consuming fire. But for unbelievers, ruinously, the fire brings destruction forever. There is one fire, but two destinies. At the Red Sea, both Egypt and Israel were baptized, but the waters destroyed only Egypt. Doesn't that tell us something? Yes, it speaks of two different destinies.

In the Bible, of course, the fires of wrath are a figure. The flames that burn up all ungodliness are the unquenchable fires of judgment that operate through God's word. God is a consuming fire (Heb. 12:29). But that is a metaphor. It means that the accomplishment of his plan does away with all that opposes it (Amos 5:6; Heb. 10:27). Fire consumes and burns. It destroys (Isa. 33:11-14). The wicked will become like ashes (Zeph. 1:18; Mal. 4:1-6). The wrath of God will burn like unquenchable fire (Jer. 4:4, 7:20, 17:27, 21:12). But it is not a literal fire, or literal wrath. What is literal is the destruction that comes by God's Word being fulfilled.

Destruction Is Forever

Eternal, unquenchable fire is a metaphor for God's judgment that lasts forever. Eternal fire destroys eternally. Its destruction has no end. But the act or process of destroying does not last forever. The nonexistence after having been destroyed is what lingers. We must not confuse the outcome of an action with the action itself. An action is not the same thing as its result. A car wreck is not the same thing as the wreck in the junkyard. Destroying and destruction, its result, are two separate and distinct ideas.

We must not be boonswoggled by tradition's game of termswitch. Destruction is a noun, not a verb. Destruction, the result of destroying, is not the same as the action that destroys. Destroying is a verb form, and is the momentary action, which has a definite end. It cannot be eternal. The quick, momentary fall of the guillotine is not identical to, nor co-extensive with, the decapitation that follows. The quick fall of the blade is over in an instant, but the headlessness lasts forever. The car crash takes but a moment, but the crushed fenders and broken lights, well, you get the point.

If something ends, it's not eternal. If it's eternal, it doesn't end. The two ideas are mutually exclusive. They wear boxing gloves. Likewise, if something is destroyed, it is not eternal. If it's eternal, then it's not destroyed. Destroying is the action or process. If the action happens forever, then its result can never be destruction. Destruction is the result of destroying. Eternal destroying is balderdash. The opposite of existence is nonexistence.

The fires of eternal destruction burn until they consume the wicked. The wicked do not burn forever. They are burnt up, destroyed, and their destruction, the result of their burning, is what lasts forever. The Bible truth is that the chaff will be burned up and destroyed with unquenchable fire (Matt. 3:12). It is not eternal. And the fire is not literal. For that matter, neither is the chaff literal. These are all just metaphors.

The destroying that happens in Hell is an action that is completed and has an end, like the quick fall of the guillotine. Its results, which are eternal destruction, are everlasting (Matt. 25:46). The destruction of the wicked means that they go into nonexistence. Their destruction will have no end (2 Thess. 1:9). They will be no more (Ps. 104:35). Eternal fire is the burning whose results, not its burning, last forever (Jude 7). This bears repeating. Unquenchable fire, a metaphor for the Word of God, burns unquenchably only until it consumes the fuel (Eze. 20:47-48). The results last forever. And the eternal fire of God's judgment and wrath is a figure. It isn't literal.

The righteous, not the unrighteous, are the ones who will live with unquenchable fire (Isa. 4:4-6, 33:14-15; Mal. 3:1-3). They can live with the outworking of God's Word. None can quench the fire of God's wrath (Amos 5:6). But what kind of loving God would remain angry forever? His wrath is just an anthropomorphism. Remember that word? God is pictured as an angry parent only so that his children can understand his will. His judgment will be eternal, but God won't continue judging the wicked forever and ever (Heb. 6:2). The game of Law is over. Jesus won. God has folded up the game board, and put the pieces back in their box.

In speaking of eternal judgment, the prophet Isaiah promised that Edom would burn, and her smoke would rise forever and ever (Isa. 34:9-15). But Edom is not eternal. What the prophet meant was that her end would be everlasting. She would cease to exist forever. The smoke is just a symbol picturing the results of her destruction, not of her continued burning. Edom was not a burning bush that will never be consumed. And the ground on which the burning bush grew was holy ground, not Hell. Eternal judgment simply means that the judgment will never be rescinded, not that the sentencing itself will drag on endlessly forever.

Likewise, eternal redemption is accomplished in a moment, but it lasts forever (Heb. 5:9, 9:12). Salvation has a start, but it continues eternally. Eternal sin is the same. It is not sinned forever (Mark 3:29). We must not confuse judgment with judging, punishment with punishing, or destruction with destroying. We must refuse the traditionalist termswitch. Hell is not the place of eternal destroying, but of destruction. Don't mix them or you'll get an explosion of error.

Eternal Worms, and Other Oddities

Nothing incites the traditionalist imagination more than to see pedestrians walk by outside its doctrine of Hell. Barking wildly, it runs at the fence of logic, growling horribly, and clawing savagely as if to get out and bite.

Hellish Maggots

One of these traditionalist barks are the strange worms from Hell that do not die. Presumably, these hellish maggots are constantly knawing and chewing on the poor wretches that inhabit the nether regions. Having insatiable appetites, they are ever eating, but for some unknown reason they are never able to finish the meal. They're never satisfied. One must wonder what kind of food the people in Hell eat, in order to replace the flesh that the worms continuously bite off. Where does such marvelous food grow? The trees in Hell must be as good as those that grow in Paradise! Or maybe they're even better, for there's more people in Hell than in heaven! Does the tree of life grow in Hell? No, the tree of life is a symbol of Christ. It does not grow in Hell.

Are the tormented people of Hell constantly eating too, like the worms? Excuse me, but I must ask. What happens to all that worm and human excrement? Yucky, yucky. Is that what Hell is?

The worms, too, if they're constantly eating, must also be constantly depositing. Otherwise, they would become ever-expanding universes of girth and gut. We're speaking of eternity here. On the other hand, perhaps they don't eat. But what's so scary about worms that don't eat? Do they tickle?

Jesus mentions these worms in a reference back to the final verse in the book of Isaiah (Mark 9:48). Worms that do not die are like the fires of judgment that are not quenched. They are merely a figure of speech, a symbol of the eternal destruction that will come upon everyone who is not united with Christ. Immortal maggots do not exist. When Christ died for the ungodly, it didn't include worms. Nor did it include demons and devils, or even the unsaved.

When Jesus mentioned maggots that do not die, he was merely citing the prophecy of Isaiah, which was clearly figurative (Isa. 14:11, 66:24). Worms, like fire, are a symbol of death and destruction (cf. Matt. 3:12). The meaning is that the wicked will be eliminated forever (Ps. 92:7).

In Bible times, dumps were kept constantly burning because people would throw dead animals, human carcasses, and other waste into these valleys and pits. In the Old Testament, one of these was called *Tophet* (Isa. 30:33). In the New Testament it was called *Gehenna,* sometimes translated in English Bibles as Hell. Unlike a house fire, these fires were not quenched because more garbage was continually being added. The carcasses and other waste were constantly crawling with maggots.

These garbage pits became a byword and symbol of unending destruction. Jesus taught, by way of example, that it was better to cut off or pluck out an offending limb or eye and enter into life, than to keep these and be cast to Gehenna. He was using figures of speech. Otherwise, we'd all have no hands or eyes, wouldn't we?

Trembling medieval minds mistook the figures for reality. They took them as proof of a literal place of eternal burning. With this mistaken belief they persecuted, maimed, and horribly tortured untold numbers of dissidents, whoever would not pay allegiance to their Church. And they passed down these nightmarish beliefs from generation to generation. Present-day churches continue to retell these horror stories as if they were true. But no, Virginia, there are no eternal maggots from Hell.

The Outer Darkness

Jesus spoke about the outer darkness as well, and in the same way of example. It was a cipher for being outside of Christ, the light of life. Traditionalists who believe in literal fires, worms, and darkness have never really explained how these could exist together in the same time and place. Worms and darkness cannot exist in literal fire. And if the fires of Hell were literal, so as to cause the poor wretches imprisoned there indescribable agony, would it not also cause the worms to suffer as much? What was their sin, to deserve such a fate? But such is the allurement of fantasy and imagination. The scarier the movie, the more crowds it draws. And eternal torture is the scariest movie of all.

On the other hand, fear is also an effective means of control. Throughout her history, the Church has sought to control both kings and commoners with the screaming fires of the outer darkness. And she succeeded much of the time.

But the outer darkness, too, is just another figure of eternal destruction. It means to be outside of the kingdom of light, excluded from Christ (Acts 26:18; Col. 1:12). Christ, of course, is the light (2 Thess. 1:9). The outer darkness is a metaphor for extinction, the absence of life and existence. It is the final result of remaining unreconciled to God in Christ.

Weeping and Gnashing of Teeth

In the common nightmare, told and retold in countless churches, the wicked gnash their teeth for pain while agonizing in Hell's ever burning fires. That's not what the Bible teaches. The gnashing of teeth is from envy and anger, not from unspeakable agonies. The wicked gnash their teeth against the righteous before the wicked melt away (Ps. 112:10). It's jealous anger directed against the righteous by the wicked (Ps. 35:16, 37:12). It's an attack by the enemies of God's people (Job 16:9; Lam. 2:16).

Remember the first Christian martyr Stephen? Before they stoned him, the Jews gnashed their teeth at him (Acts 7:54). It didn't happen in Hell, or in the outer darkness, or in the scorching throes of unquenchable pain. It happened at Jerusalem. And their smoke was not literally rising, was it?

The gnashing of teeth of which Jesus spoke does not last forever. It happens at the Judgment, not in the unquenchable fires of an everlasting Hell (Luke 13:28). It happens as the wicked see themselves cast unto destruction, while the righteous are blessed with all the bounty that heaven can offer. The Biblical gnashing of teeth is an act of animal savagery against the righteous. It doesn't happen in Hell, it doesn't last forever, and it's not a response to unbearable pain. Not much of the tradition is true, is it?

The Lake of Fire and Brimstone

The lake of fire and brimstone that John saw in his vision is sometimes identified with Hell. But that, too, reveals a clouded understanding. The Revelation tells its tale with symbols. The sea or lake of fire is really a symbol of humanity under God's judgment (Rev. 17:15). Seas symbolize peoples (Jer. 6:23, 50:42; Dan. 7:2f). They rage and storm, tossed back and forth by the various winds of doctrine and ideology. The Dragon, a symbol of Satan, lives in this sea (Isa. 27:1). He lives in the hearts of the peoples.

Surprisingly, the lake of fire is also the sea of glass before the throne of God, upon which the saints are seen standing. Its solid, crystalline surface keeps the saints from sinking. It's a picture of the saints' victory over their own carnal human nature and death. This same sea of crystal reappears later as a lake mingled with fire, and then as the lake of fire and brimstone (Rev. 4:6, 15:2, 19:20, 20:15). It's the same lake, but now it's a symbol of rebellious humanity suffering the judgments of God. Unlike the saints, the wicked cannot walk on water, and they sink forever into its boiling depths. They sink and are burned up in the judgments of God. But his judging will not last forever. And the sea is not the H-word.

The symbols show that the hot fires of judgment will burn up the wicked, leaving the saints unharmed. The saints will walk on water as on glass, exultant in their resurrection bodies, free from danger of sinking into its awful plagues. But, like the world of Noah's day, and the Egyptian army of the Exodus, the rest of humanity will be swallowed up by these deadly waters of humanity and will be destroyed. They will cease to exist, for in the new world there will be no more sea (Rev. 21:1). It will have dried up (Isa. 51:9; Jer. 51:36-37). The lake of fire and brimstone, a symbol of humanity figuratively burning under judgment, does not last forever (Isa. 34:9-10). Its fires die out when humanity is destroyed. And Death and Hell are thrown into the lake as well. Good riddance. They share in the fate of the wicked.

The eternal torment of the Devil, the Beast, and the False Prophet in this lake does not mean conscious pain forever either. It symbolizes the permanence of God's fiery judgment. The lake burns. Burning is destruction. Brimstone is a symbol of the burning coals reeking with the foul stench of sinfulness as it is burnt (Isa. 30:33). It too, is just a symbol (Isa. 34:1-17). The fire, the brimstone, and the lake itself are all of them symbolic, as is the entire book of Revelation (Rev. 9:17-18). The destruction formerly of Sodom and Gomorrah by fire and brimstone prefigures this lake's fires of destruction (Gen. 19:24-25; Jude 7). Those cities were destroyed. They do not still burn. Get it? Destruction, not destroying, is forever.

The Beast thrown to these fires of God's eternal judgment is not an individual person. Beasts are symbols of governments and kingdoms (Rev. 17:3, 9-10). A government, of course, is not alive, or conscious, and cannot suffer pain. In the lake it goes to destruction, not to unending agony (Dan. 7:26; Rev. 17:11). Governments don't feel pain, child. They haven't a real body. Nor do churches. Both institutions are just ideas, just communal ideas, remember?

The False Prophet is the apostate ecumenical Christian Church of the End-time, head-quartered in Rome (Rev. 18:4, 21). Churches and religious organizations, like governments, have no nerve endings, and can't suffer pain. They are bodiless, for they are really just communal ideas. Neither of these institutions is truly alive or conscious. The casting of Satan and the two beasts into the lake means they will be destroyed forever, along with humanity. The Serpent will die with Adam (Gen. 3:14-19). The lake of fire is the second death, the death of the spirit (Rev. 20:14). The death of the spirit cannot be another separation. The second death is the dissolution of the individual spirit.

Sheol and Hades

Sheol is an Old Testament Hebrew word sometimes translated as Hell. It means the all-receiving grave, imagined as a place underground (Ps. 139:8; Isa. 38:10). Hades, too, like Gehenna, is also sometimes translated as Hell. It's a New Testament Greek word that means the unseen, or the grave. It, too, is metaphorically a place where the dead go to await judgment. Sheol and Hades are both the same place, the temporary abode of the dead. They're a holding tank for spirits.

In the Revelation, Hades and Death are personified as horsemen, Hades following after Death. Both are eventually cast into the lake of fire and brimstone (Rev. 6:8, 20:14). But neither of them is a real person, so they cannot be consciously tormented. Death is not a person, and cannot suffer pain. And Hades is a place. It, too, cannot be literally tormented. If it were Hell, and the lake of fire is Hell, the whole thing becomes nonsense. It would mean that Hell is thrown into itself. The dog chasing its own tail finally catches it and swallows himself? Are we talking eternal indigestion here? And what about Death? He's a personification, not a real person. Will death literally suffer forever? No, these are just symbols. Don't let their masks scare you, little one.

Before the cross, there were in Sheol both righteous and unrighteous persons (Dan. 12:2). Jacob and David went there (Gen. 42:38; Ps. 16:10). Jesus himself went into Sheol (Jonah 2:2; Acts 2:27, 31). He opened its gates and released its captives (Eph. 1:20-21,

4:8-9). He holds its keys (Rev. 1:18). Only the wicked remain there, awaiting judgment (Rev. 20:13). People who die in Christ go into God's presence (Eccl. 12:7; Luke 23:43; John 12:26, 17:24; Acts 7:59; 2 Cor. 5:1, 8; Phil. 1:21-23; 1 Thess. 4:14). Death holds no nightmares for the saints.

Lazarus and Dives

In Greek thought there were two areas in Hades. One was Elysium, where the righteous dwelt. The other was Tartarus, the region of the unrighteous. And there was a great gulf between the two. In Hebrew thought there were likewise two areas in Sheol. One was Paradise or Abraham's bosom, where the righteous dead awaited the Judgment. The other was Gehenna. Jesus' story of the rich man and Lazarus involves these two places within Hades (Luke 16:19-31). The rich man was in Gehenna, and Lazarus (Eleazar) was in Abraham's bosom. Both were in Hades.

Neither of these is the place of eternal torture called Hell. This latter is the eternal state, the place of eternal destruction. Hades, on the other hand, is just a holding tank where dead spirits await the Judgment (Rev. 20:13). Nothing is said about the rich man's torment, or for that matter Lazarus' blessedness, being eternal. Nor is there any indication that the flames are literal. As we saw earlier, fire is a symbol of the Word of God accomplishing itself. And Lazarus is carried, bodily, into Abraham's Bosom. That's in Hades, not heaven. Both men are in Hades, the temporary place of the dead.

Jesus was using popular beliefs to make a point in speaking with the Pharisees. He was contrasting two viewpoints about worldly wealth. One was that of the Jews, and especially of the

Pharisees, who mistakenly viewed worldly riches as evidence of God's blessing and favor. The other was of the spiritual man, Jesus himself, true High Priest of Israel, poor in the things of this world but having heaven's favor. True blessedness, he teaches, comes by receiving God's Word. The word of the Law and the Prophets was available. Indeed, it was standing right there in front of them! If the Jews did not believe these, neither would they believe when Jesus arose from the dead. Not believing God's word, they would miss out on the true blessings. For the true riches, they must receive God's Word. They must receive Christ.

But tragically, they did not believe the Scriptures, which spoke of him. Their understanding was darkened, like the churches of today. And like many churches of today they preferred worldly riches and prosperity rather than the Gospel of service and self-sacrifice. The teaching of the parable is that they could avoid Gehenna, the place and destiny of the wicked, by believing the Scriptures, which speak of him, the very Word of God incarnate standing there. But tragically, like today's churches they did not understand the figurative nature of the Scriptures.

Nothing is said here about either eternal salvation or Hell. It's all about the intermediate state called Hades. Jesus tells the story in past tense, before the cross and the Last Judgment. Jesus had not yet died, or gone to Hades. Upon his death he would empty Paradise. But that was still future. The parable holds no evidence whatever for the traditional nightmare.

Eternal Fires of Holiness

God is like a consuming fire, holy and separate from this world. His holiness burns up all that is unholy. Holiness separates God and his followers from the present, carnal world of sin. God's extreme sanctity was displayed on the cross, which was the true altar of holiness. The cross is a rejection of this world and its passing lusts in favor of the eternal glory. It is the supreme separation of humanity from this world, to be reconciled with God. The cross did away finally with the sinfulness of carnal existence, which is separation from the Creator. The holiness of the cross is separation from this world and a return to God.

Holiness rejects this world and receives Christ. It takes up his cross and carries it to Calvary once more. This is the fire of judgment that Jesus lit two thousand years ago (Luke 12:49-50; Rev. 8:1-6). The testimony of Jesus was fully expressed in the purifying flames of Calvary's altar. The cross is the burning testimony of Christ. It still burns, like a searing, scorching fire.

It cannot be quenched. Its coals still glow, and its flame still dances in the faithful Gospel preaching and dying of the saints. The word of their faithful testimony, and their own cross that takes them out of this world of darkness, is the holy fire that will engulf the world fully in the final conflagration. It's the fiery baptism that John foretold, that will express God's absolute holiness, and his purpose for this world. The saints' testimony in Christ that is spreading everywhere is the hot, eternal fire that sanctifies. This world will burn, and a bright new world will form from its ashes, a new world sanctified by its separation from this present corruption. The testimony of Christ is the living Word of God, and it cannot be quenched. Let it burn unquenched in your heart, child.

Chapter FIVE

A Mathematical Mistake

Three Equals One, They Say

Perhaps the most misunderstood doctrine in the long tradition of misinterpretations is the tradition of the Trinity. No other doctrine was debated so widely, and over a longer period.

It was developed over many years by Church councils convened from all over Christendom. These councils were so rife with intrigues, threats, and murders that the Emperor of Rome finally had to intervene in one case and declare who would prevail. The Roman Catholic dogma of the Trinity, which the Protestant churches have received from her, did not develop from Bible truths or from Spirit-led teachings of the first Christians. It came from later political machinations and power struggles, clearly not the fruit of the Spirit. The doctrine is illogical and satanic, as we'll see.

With the blinders of fanaticism over her eyes, and accusations of heresy on her lips, the Church murdered any who refused her Trinitarian creed. Today, loyal churchmen still wear those blinders. Even Protestants become inquisitors and cry "Heresy!" against whoever refuses to kneel before this three-headed idol. But the true character of this dogma is revealed by its birth and parentage. It is not the fruit of the Spirit.

The Trinity is the brainchild of churchmen trying to accommodate Christian theology to Greek thought. It attempts to harmonize the immutable, aloof and wholly other god of Greek philosophy with the creative, dynamic and involved God of the Hebrews who desires that all may know him (Hos. 2:20; 1 Cor. 13:12; 1 John 2:27). It's a fantasy marriage of Zeus with Yahweh. And it's an impossibility.

Not only is this asinine doctrine historically the most debated, it's also the most incomprehensible and illogical among a crowd of illogical and unscriptural doctrines. With the Trinity, irrationality reaches new heights. Nonsense is elevated to divinity, and worshippers are induced-or coerced-to kneel and worship at the foot of absurdity and, as we shall see, blasphemy.

Indeed, its very absurdity is inanely touted as proof of its truth. Supposedly, the notion must be true because it is so absurd! The Trinity's incomprehensibility supposedly proves God's transcendence and unknowability. It verifies that God is much too high for human comprehension. He is beyond the capacity of mere human language to capture. Sincere churchmen imagine, then, that the best way to describe and honor God is to say that he is absurd! Irrationality is their highest accolade. They revel in God's incoherence! Illogic is the proof of God! It's insane.

Indeed, since he so transcends description, they even describe him sometimes as silence and darkness, absolutely beyond what we can say or imagine. They say this as if they knew what he is like. He is indescribable, they say, describing him. Huh? True believers do not worship the unknown god. They do not indulge in such idolatry. We do not sing and pray to darkness and silence. God is light and truth, and he speaks, in his word and in our hearts (John 14:6; 1 Cor. 2:10-16). And he wants us to know him.

Jesus was the Word that God sent to his people to reveal and communicate himself. He was the Light that makes God known (John 1:18, 14:6-9; 1 Cor. 13:12). He revealed God. To stubbornly insist that God is unknowable is to oppose his will, deny his word, and spit in the face of Christ. How do they know he's unknowable, if he's unknowable? Their claim that God is unknowable is their admission that they don't know him! God is not the great Silence. He speaks, loudly and clearly. He is not the great Darkness, but the great Light that illumines the hearts and minds of his people. The doctrine of the Trinity that the churches shake before us is not a baby rattle. It's the tail end of a live rattlesnake!

The Oneness of God

The doctrine maintains that God is and has always been simultaneously one, yet three, and three, yet one. He is one substance, three Persons, from all eternity. Each is fully God, not one-third of him, but all of God. Each (each?) may have a unique function, but with no distinction or division in essence. When one of the three acts, all three are fully present.

Mysteriously, each of the three Persons can have distinct personal attributes and function with no distinction in nature, essence, or being. And although the Spirit and the Son may freely subject themselves to the Father, this does not imply inferiority. Accordingly, they are different and unequal, but not different, and not unequal. Each is God complete. Together they are not greater than each singly. Singly, they are not less than all three together. Huh? How do they know this?

Baby Jesus was fully God from his conception. Mary, then, was the Mother of God. God himself entered her virgin womb to become flesh, grow to manhood, and suffer death. Jesus' suffering was God's suffering. At the cross, nevertheless, the Father forsook the Son. Jesus died forsaken, separated from himself. Through it all, God remained immutable, unchanged and inseparably merged. The doctrine is hopelessly irrational. But don't take that as proof of God's greatness, child. It's proof of human stupidity.

The God of Israel

The Trinitarian conception of God runs counter to the central belief of Judaism. In Judaism, God is One, and only One (Deut. 6:4). He is singular, and simple. There is no divine plurality. There is only one God, and he will not share his divine glory or Personhood with any created thing (Isa. 42:8). For the Jews, the Christian idea of God is idolatrous.

Yahweh alone is the true God and Sovereign of the universe. To make an image or likeness, or a substitute for him, reeks of idolatry and falsehood, and is strictly forbidden. There is none like God, and there never will be (Isa. 43:10-12). It was because Jesus claimed sonship from God, that the Jews attempted to stone him (John 8:58-59, 10:30-33). The God of Israel is one Lord, and there is none like him. All other gods are idols.

Moreover, in Judaism God in his nature is completely distinct from the creation. He is utterly holy, thrice-told. The First Commandment prohibits worship of any created thing. Judaism rejects the notion that a human could be God, of the same substance as the Creator. That which is of the earth is earthly. That which is of heaven is heavenly. The two may interact, but they do not mix. The creature and the Creator are essentially and diametrically different from one another and must be kept forever separate, for

God is absolutely holy. And he's a jealous God, easily provoked to wrath, so be careful.

The Three-ness of God

Christianity responds with the claim to worship this same God of Israel too, but from a more developed and informed understanding, since revelation is progressive. As the New Testament shows, the Christian God is One, yes, but he is also Three. He is one God in three Persons. This is the sticking point between the two religions. In Judaism, if God is One, he cannot be three. A singular God composed of three Persons, all fully God, of the same substance, co-equal, co-eternal and without division among them, is just not possible. Three is always and forever plural. Three persons means three gods. Three does not equal one. It's just not possible.

Christians answer that human understanding is limited, and God is far beyond our comprehension. But he has revealed himself as Father, Son, and Holy Spirit. It's as if the one God of Israel reveals himself three ways: left side, right side, and full face. He exists in three Persons beyond human capacity to understand, because that is how he is revealed in Scripture. They point out that, even in the Jewish Old Testament, there are hints that God is plural (Gen. 1:26; Isa. 6:8). The root of the word used for God's oneness means a uniting, and hints that God is complex.

In the Bible, Christians passionately claim, God is both singular and plural. The Father, Son, and Spirit are all three of them God, even though God is one. We must accept illogic and irrationality when it applies to God, because that's how he has revealed himself in the New Testament. We must not question the Church. Rather than demonstrate our stupidity, it proves our faith!

Wrong Inferences

Does this doctrine that defies reason and logic really arise from Scripture, or is it a misinterpretation? The matter is not unimportant. We must not commit idolatry by worshipping the wrong God. Do we worship all three Persons, or just the Father? Should we pray to Jesus? Should we accept God's unknowability and irrationality on pure faith? What is the truth of the Trinity?

By all admission, the doctrine is not explicitly taught in the Bible. It is an inference drawn from various passages, along with other supporting doctrines. But are these inferences truth, or false inferences? As we've seen so far, the tradition is fraught with error. Might this be an exception? Let's look and see.

How Could God Be Human?

We can start by realizing that the references in the Old Testament to the singular and plural nature of the one God were figures that point forward. The things of the Law and the Prophets are foreshadowings of the reality that is to be made real in Christ. The things of the Old Testament look expectantly to him for their certain fulfillment. And shockingly for church traditionalists, even the revelation of God in the Old Testament is but a figure that will be fulfilled and made manifest in Christ. The Old Testament God will be fully revealed only in the fullness of Christ. The Old Testament God is just a shadow!

As in the Old Testament, the New Testament teaches that there is only one God (1 Tim. 2:5; Jas. 2:19). This is true even when Christ is Lord along with the Spirit and the Father (1 Cor. 8:4-6). The inference, then, is that all three, being God, must in some sense be identical. Although there is a oneness to God, there is also a plurality. There is a threeness to God.

Moreover, if Christ is God, then he must be eternal, and must possess the full array of attributes that God has possessed from all eternity. He must be omniscient, omnipotent, omnipresent, and possess all the other divine omni's. He must be God in the fullest sense. And this must be true of him from all eternity. We may ask, then, how could the human Jesus, who was flesh and very obviously not omnipresent or eternal, be divine? How could God be flesh?

Did God Empty Himself? (Phil. 2:5-11)

Tradition's answer, which is taken from Paul's letter to the Philippians, is that God emptied himself of his attributes, laying them aside when he took on flesh (Phil. 2:5-11). But that is an oxymoron, a self-contradiction, and a misinterpretation. And it actually denies the Trinity. Is an empty God really God? The smell of illogic is quite strong here.

The passage in Philippians is an exhortation to love one another, to be of humble mind and demeanor like Christ Jesus. It includes the saints. Got that? The point is that our attitude and spirit should be like that of Christ. However, in our Bibles Trinitarians have translated this passage and its true meaning is obscured (Phil. 2:5-11). A loose translation might be as follows:

> "Have this mind in you, which was also in Christ Jesus who, coming to be in the form of God, thought it not robbery to be the same as God, but emptied himself, taking the form of a servant, made in the likeness of men. And being found in the form of a man, he humbled

> himself, becoming obedient unto death, even death on a cross. Therefore God highly exalted him, and granted him the name above all names, so that at the name of Jesus every knee in heaven and on earth and under the earth should bow, and every tongue should confess that Jesus Christ is Lord, to the glory of God the Father."
> (The author's translation taken from The Greek New Testament, United Bible Societies, 1983)

Looking closely, we can see that the passage says nothing about preexistence, incarnation, birth, the Trinity, or any other ideas that Trinitarians try to inject into it. It says that we should have the same attitude or manner of thinking as did Christ Jesus. We should be like him.

Are we to have the same attitude as a fetus? Are we to think like a divine molecule? No, this passage refers to Jesus the full-grown man (Matt. 20:28). It's not about his supposed incarnation in Mary's womb. Should we then strive to have the attitude of a pre-existent, incomprehensible deity? You know the answer.

Jesus was a man born about 2,000 years ago, not in eternity. This is not an impossible exhortation to have the same attitude as a fetus or a molecule or a preexistent deity! Paul says that this man Jesus came to exist in the form/nature of God, and did not consider it rapine to be equal to/similar to/like God. And we must have the same attitude! We should have the same attitude of a man who found himself to have the nature of God himself. The exhortation is to Christ-likeness. It says we should be like Christ!

Then he says that Jesus emptied or humbled himself. How? It was not by a pre-existent deity being born, but by taking the form/likeness of a servant. He abased himself by becoming a servant.

This says nothing about being born, or about incarnation, or about God taking off his attributes, a nonsensical idea. It says he humbled himself by becoming a servant, not that God emptied himself by being born as a human baby. And he shared in the likeness of men.

Now, it's true that men may sometimes act like babies, but acting and being are two different animals. Men are not babies, no matter their actions. And men are not born. Babies are born. And anyway, this passage is about the man Christ Jesus, who definitely did not act like a baby.

In verse seven, the word is a form of *lambano*. It means to take, assume, or receive. It doesn't mean to be born. And it's in active voice. If it referred to his birth, it would mean that Jesus birthed himself as a servant. That's twaddle. Newborn babies are not born as servants, and servants are not born. It was Mary, not a preexistent Jesus, who conceived and birthed him. It doesn't say he emptied himself by becoming a sperm! Nor are sperms servants, nor do they look like men!

In Matthew 26:26, Jesus took bread. Is this a hint that he was born as a loaf of bread, or that he birthed himself as bread? In Revelation 5:7, the Lamb took the book. A book was born! Is that not nonsense? This passage does not deal with Jesus' birth, or his gestation period, or a supposed pre-existence as God.

This passage tells us that, although Jesus came to share in divinity, he didn't see this as an excuse for pride or self-service, or for lording it over others. His divinity was not something for which he needed to grab. It was his. Nevertheless, he remained humble and obedient even to the extreme of dying a tortured death by crucifixion. Because of his humble faithfulness, which is an example for us, God granted him entrance to the highest glory, which is complete inviolate oneness with himself. Jesus is now Lord in the fullest sense of the word. He is now fully and completely one and the same with God.

Astonishingly, the passage exhorts us to follow his example! We must have the same attitude that Christ Jesus manifested, for the same reasons. Clearly, we can't have an attitude of Christ-like humility unless we are Christ-like. Mere human humility is not Christ-like! And in order to have this attitude like his of divine humility we must be divine! We must be like him (John 10:34-35, 17:21-23; Heb. 2:10-11; 2 Peter 1:4; etc.)!

But we too, like him, must not let our new, divine nature become an excuse for lording it over others. We must remain faithful to our ministry of service, and God will receive us into the same inviolate Oneness in which Christ and the Father now share! There's no proof of an eternally existent Trinity here. It's strong evidence of our glorious and exalted standing in Christ. We are Children of God!

The traditional understanding is that the Son, the second Person of the Trinity, emptied himself of his divine attributes in becoming flesh at his conception. But this passage does not deal with his conception. It deals with his adulthood. Nor does it deal with divine attributes. Having become divine, he nevertheless found himself in the form of a man. Finding himself as a man, not as a sperm or baby, he became a servant. He humbled himself and was obedient even to the point of dying on the cross.

None of these things happened at his conception. And they surely didn't happen before his conception, as if a collection of divine atoms, humble though they may be, came together to form a sperm that joined up with a human ovum. Such an idea is beyond rationality. And most importantly, he is an example that we should follow. Get it? We must have the same attitude, and expect the same outcome. Think about it, child. The passage actually exhorts the saints to be like Christ! It's not just about humility, but about divine humility! Just remember that it's also about suffering and service. It hints that we too have a cross to bear.

What the passage tells us, is that although Jesus came to partake of divinity when, as we know, he received the seal of the Spirit immediately after his baptism, he didn't get a swelled head over it. He stayed true to his ministry, and fulfilled his calling. Because of his exemplary faithfulness, God graciously exalted him into the fullness of the supreme glory, giving him the name above all names. And the saints should have that same attitude, for the same reward!

Clearly, this passage rejects the traditional doctrine of a co-equal, co-eternal Trinity, of a Son who is as old as his Father. It doesn't proclaim an absurd God with three heads that are actually one head who is infinitely above and beyond us. It emphatically rejects the notion that God is immutable and unchanging as well. It says that Jesus is Lord, not that the Trinity is Lord. Jesus the man, the human who died and rose again, is Lord. And we can be like him! If we can be like Christ Jesus, and he became divine through Spirit baptism, then we too become divine through the same baptism. We become One with God. It teaches that we should not get swelled heads about it, not that we should develop three heads! We should be like Jesus.

The attitude to which he calls us is servanthood, even while being fully conscious that we share with Christ Jesus in the divine nature. It's a call to Christ-likeness. To change this godly, Christ-like humility to which Paul exhorts us into mere human humility, denying that we share in the divine nature, is a rejection of Paul's exhortation, as well as of the Gospel. To pretend that mere human humility is Christ-like distorts its meaning and is just plain rebellion and disobedience. And disobedience is like witchcraft (1 Sam. 15:22-23). And witchcraft is an abomination.

But what happened to the Trinity? Is/are he/they hiding somewhere? Let's look at some other passages. Maybe we can find him/them.

Other Passages and True Interpretations

God's Radiance of Glory (Heb. 1:1-12)

In this passage, the Son is said to be the radiance of God's glory, the exact expression of his divine nature, the One through whom God created the ages or worlds. Moreover, he upholds all things by his empowered Word, sitting at the right hand of the throne of supreme Majesty. He is the Son and appointed Heir to all things, superior even to the angels. Surely, then, he must be fully divine.

Yes, exactly! The man Christ Jesus is divine. He is Lord of lords and King of kings. The passage speaks about the present. It says that he is now, presently, the radiance of God's glory and nature. But it was only after he made purification for sins that he sat down in this place of supreme Majesty on high. He *became* better than the angels by *inheriting* a name superior to theirs. It was not his from all eternity. He inherited it. He was appointed unto the honor. It happened in history, not in the nameless past.

Jesus the man, born of human womb, inherited the name of God in his baptism in the Spirit, for which the celestial voice acknowledged him as God's beloved Son. The Father declared that he had begotten Jesus on that very day, when he anointed him King in Zion (Ps. 2:1-12).

He was appointed heir, and received sonship and the inheritance because of his faithfulness. These were not his from all eternity. They were given him. He was made better than the angels by inheriting a better name. This all happened in partial fashion at the Jordan. It reached its fullness after he had made purification for sins. When he sat down at the right hand of the Majesty on high, it was after fulfilling his ministry. It was after the cross (Heb. 10:11-13). He was elevated to that seat of honor after his willing death. Now he is Lord, the radiance of God's glory, and the exact expression of God himself. He received all these things. They were not his from all eternity. This passage, too, rejects a co-equal, co-eternal Trinity.

Jesus is superior to the angels, it says, because unlike them, he is called God's Son. He inherited a name and nature above that of angels. It was inherited, not his from all eternity. The coming Messiah, or Christ, was to be God's Son (Mark 14:61). Jesus became the Christ, and God's Son, when he received the Spirit. He was begotten not in eternity, a ridiculous thought, but beside the flowing currents of the Jordan river. He now sits on the throne of greatness and glory, that is, in the seat of God. But he didn't sit there until after he had made purification for sins.

Elsewhere, we find that the saints share in these same honors. They, too, are called Sons of God (Ps. 82:6; 1 John 3:1-2). They, too, share in the throne of highest Majesty (Eph. 1:20, 2:6; Rev. 3:21). Yes, we have inherited a name and nature superior to angels! We share in the Oneness of God. He has moved over on the throne to make room for us. Our inheritance is to share in Christ. It's glorious. Don't let anyone steal your glory, child!

I and the Father Are One (John 10:30)

In this passage, Jesus' claim of oneness with the Father was really a claim to divinity. For this seeming sacrilege, the Jews intended to stone him. In their closed minds, and in their darkened doctrine, humanity and divinity were irreconcilably separate. Does that remind you of anyone, child? In answer, Jesus explained that his oneness with the Father was a union in the Spirit (John 10:30-39). He is hinting of his baptism in the Spirit. The religious leaders saw his words as blasphemy, but their own false and rigidly loyalist conceptions were the true blasphemy. Many Trinitarians today would follow zealously in their footsteps. See the stones in their hands?

They would bring the same charge of blasphemy against God's children today, against every saint who refuses to bow down before the three-headed idol they have fashioned and placed in the churches. Many churchmen insist the saints are God's children only metaphorically, by an imaginary adoption, and not like Jesus. He was unique, the God-man, and forever different from ordinary humans, forever above and beyond us, they say. In fact, God is an absurdity, they swear in all seriousness and with much aplomb. But that is most assuredly not what Jesus taught.

Soon after his anointing, Satan attacked Jesus' sonship (Luke 4:3). Did Spirit baptism really make him God's Son? The Serpent's insinuations were not aimed at Jesus' identification within an eternal Trinity of Father, Son, and Spirit, nor at Jesus' human conception and birth. The point of attack was the meaning and efficacy of his baptism. The bull's-eye was his anointing which had just recently happened. Satan questioned Jesus' sonship, his priesthood, and his kingship, all the result of his reception of the

Spirit of Christ. How was a mere human, even if anointed, truly God's son?

Satan's three arrows were aimed at the events recently transpired, not at what had happened thirty years earlier in Nazareth. This is more evidence that Jesus became the Son of God in his anointing by the Spirit, while he was still dripping with Jordan's cold waters. Jesus, like us, received the Spirit. Is he not our divine pattern that we are called to follow?

You Have Seen the Father (John 14:9)

Jesus said that the disciples had in fact seen the Father in seeing him. Again, rather than being evidence for a Trinity, this meant that the Spirit was in him, and he in the Spirit (John 14:10-11). He and the Spirit were now One, a shared identity. He and the Father were now one because he had received the Spirit. In fact, when the Spirit comes upon his disciples they too will participate in that same oneness (John 14:20). Both he and the Father will come and make their abode in every true disciple who keeps his words (John 14:23). They must abide in him, and he will abide in them and will produce godly fruit (John 15:4). But like him, they will suffer persecution for it (John 15:18-21). Trinitarians are not beyond casting stones in defense of their three-headed idol.

Jesus didn't say that he and the Father are Three. His oneness with God was not an eternal three-ness. It was a new relationship in which his disciples, too, could participate. Like him, they are not of this world (John 15:19, 17:16). Their glory is oneness with him and with the Father (John 17:21-23). His glory is their glory! This is the same glory that the Word, now become the Son, had with the Father before the world was (John 17:5, 22-24). In the beginning, the Word was with God, and was God. And the Word became flesh, in Jesus. And Jesus' experience of Sonship was the example and pattern for the Sonship of the saints! Remember what following an example means? It means that we are expected to be like him. Hallelujah! We are to be like Jesus!

Jesus was displaying the saints' incredible future right before their very eyes. His destiny is their destiny, he says. His life is their life. His glory is the very glory in which the saints will share. They will receive Sonship in the very same manner as he had, by rebirth from on high (John 3:5). And it will be of like kind as the Sonship of Christ Jesus. He is the firstfruits. They will follow. The rest of the crop will be like him.

Additionally, he frankly admits that it is cause for rejoicing that he goes to the Father, because the Father was greater than he (John 14:28). Can it be said any plainer? Jesus was looking to receive things even greater and more marvelous than what he possessed (Heb. 12:2-3). The cross was the doorway into the holy of holies, into which he would soon enter. Suffering and death were his path unto the fullness of eternal glory.

This passage is a strong, clear refutation of the doctrine of the Trinity from the lips of Jesus himself. If he was inferior to the Father in any respect whatsoever, then the Trinity is dissolved. Beyond Calvary exaltation beckoned. He was not yet the fullness of God, but he soon would be. And he is the firstfruits, first of a vast, unnumbered and abundant harvest that would follow him all the way to glory and beyond. That's what firstfruits means. It means that there will be more like him.

The Word Was God (John 1:1-3)

John begins his Gospel as a sort of new Genesis, with the divine Word who was in the beginning with God. In the man Jesus, this divine Word had become flesh. The critical issue is when that occurred. Was it at his conception, or at the Jordan? John's answer is that it was at the Jordan.

It's true, as we saw earlier, that the Word causes matter to take the form of flesh in every human through the natural laws and processes of generation. This world was, after all, fabricated through the Word. In this sense, the word spoken to Mary by the angel was fulfilled and became flesh when she conceived Jesus virginally by the Spirit's empowerment. It continued becoming flesh, naturally, throughout Jesus' life. Importantly, though, John here is talking about the time when his disciples beheld Jesus' glory (John 1:14, 2:11). They saw his glory manifested while they were with him during Jesus' ministry, not at his conception. In this passage, and throughout his Gospel, John is speaking of Jesus' adulthood, of his Sonship. He's dealing with Jesus' ministry after his baptism in the Spirit.

In another, corresponding passage, John repeats this same idea, that the Word was manifested in the world (1 John 1:1-3). The eternal life that was with the Father in the beginning was revealed in the flesh. John had heard, seen, and touched this Word of life. Both passages deal, then, with John's association and experience with Jesus during Jesus' adult ministry. They do not refer to Jesus' physical birth as a baby in Bethlehem.

It is absolutely true that the creative Word was divine, and existed in the beginning with God. And this divine Word was made flesh in the man Jesus. The same Word creates the flesh of every human in the natural course of generation and growth. The creation is God's Word causing everything to take form, dressing the creation with time and place, and flesh and blood, in the natural course of things (John 1:1-3; Col. 1:17).

But John is speaking of a greater birth. And Jesus is the prime example. The destiny of Jesus is the destiny of every child of God. Jesus is the first, the leader and guide into our incredible future. The Word entered the world anew in Jesus, in order to reconcile the world back to God. And that world includes us. Jesus is the Firstborn of heaven. There will be more like him, born in the flesh naturally and then reborn in the flesh through the direct influence of God. This rebirth is what John is concerned with, the birth from above.

John is speaking of humans becoming children of God (John 1:12-13). In fact, a major purpose of the whole Gospel of John is to show that the destiny of Jesus is the example for every saint. Like Jesus, they too can become children of God. And he concludes with Christ's word to Peter, "Follow me." Believers in Christ share his nature and destiny. In none of these passages is there an eternal Trinity present.

In fact, the evangelist is explicit in saying that John the Baptist's ministry was to announce the coming of the true Light which was coming into the world (John 1:9). The coming of the Light happens after John's ministry that prepared the way. It was not, then, at Jesus' birth. The Incarnation of the Word came about at Jesus' baptism, during the ministry of John the Baptist.

Sonship Through Spirit Baptism (John 3:1-8)

Humans become Sons of God as they receive the Word of God, the Spirit of Christ, and the new birth. Upon their reception of Christ through the Spirit, they are begotten from above (John

3:1-8). This is what John is intimating repeatedly with respect to Jesus, in the first few chapters of his Gospel. Jesus became the Son of God by receiving the Spirit.

After beginning with the divinity of the Word, John stresses that the Word became flesh, and gave the same authority to become children of God to any who would receive the Word. Then immediately he tells of Jesus' exemplary baptism and John's witness (John 1:14-15, 19-34). He ignores Jesus' physical birth. But he tells us emphatically that John the Baptist testified that Jesus was the Son of God because of what happened at the Jordan (John 1:32, 34). Jesus' sonship was undeniably the result of receiving the Spirit. And we know that Jesus received the Spirit at his baptism.

Yes, it may sound strange to our ears, accustomed to tradition, but the truth is that Jesus himself received Christ. He too, like every other person who receives Christ, became the Son of God through Spirit baptism. John is showing that Jesus' divine sonship was the result of his reception of the Spirit. His sonship was expressed in his adulthood, not at his conception or childhood. It was during his ministry that he was the only-begotten Son of God (John 1:14). There is no evidence here of an eternal Trinity. In fact, it shows that God will have an innumerable number of children. Christ was the Firstborn of an untold number of humans who will be given the authority and power to become the Children of God (Heb. 2:11). No, Virginia, there is no co-equal, co-eternal Trinity here in this passage either.

Bread from Heaven (John 6:31, 33, 38)

In his discourses with the Jews, Jesus declared that he had come down from heaven. They were from below, while he was from above (John 8:23). Obviously, he was not speaking of his humanity. The man Jesus was not together in heaven with the Creator in the beginning. What did he mean, then?

When Jesus claimed to have proceeded forth and come from God, he was speaking of himself in union with the Spirit within him (John 8:42, 15:26). In that sense, he even existed before Abraham (John 8:58). Clearly, Jesus' human body did not exist before the patriarch. Even the Baptist was older than Jesus (John 1:15). But the Word of God infused with the Spirit was from the beginning. This divine Word was made flesh in a special way when Jesus was baptized in the super glue of the Spirit, and bonded permanently.

Jesus is not saying that his oneness with the Father is the result of his physical conception. He was the only-begotten of the Father during his ministry (John 1:14). The Spirit came down from heaven at the Jordan, when he alighted on Jesus. This human flesh became the fulfillment of the figure of bread from heaven. He was not literal bread. Nor did his flesh come down from heaven. Jesus didn't cry out that the sky was falling. Bread from heaven is merely a figure. It symbolizes the life through the Spirit that Jesus brought to everyone who will receive him (John 6:48-58). God gave the world this one-of-a-kind Son to provide life everlasting (John 3:16).

His ministry, he said, was to accomplish the will of the Father (John 6:38-40). The Father's will was that the Son grant eternal life to everyone that would believe in him. He and the Spirit were now one. In receiving the Spirit they would receive him. And because he was flesh and blood, in receiving the Spirit they would be partaking of his flesh and blood. And he accomplished that ministry through the cross. It would be memorialized in the Lord's Supper. And he would raise them up from death.

He is speaking from his place and authority in union with the Spirit, not just from his mere humanity. Indeed, this same Spirit would raise him up from the tomb (Rom. 8:11). When Jesus spoke of his past existence in heaven, he was speaking of himself united with the Spirit within him. His flesh and the Spirit were now of one identity. The divine Spirit had come to join with human flesh.

Jesus' absolutely marvelous message is that we're included in this same glorious destiny, joined in the Spirit with him (1 Cor. 6:17). We share the same Father, being born of the same Spirit (Luke 8:21; John 20:17; Heb. 2:11, 17; Rev. 21:7). We too, everyone born of him, are Children of God like him (Heb. 2:14, 17). Jesus is the forerunner, our great pathfinder into the holy place of God's innermost being (Heb. 6:20). He is the door into heaven (Rev. 4:1-2). We, too, will enter and know even as we are known (Rom. 8:29). We shall share fully in the divine nature, and be like him (Rom. 8:29; 2 Peter 1:4; 1 John 3:1-2). This is our breathtaking destiny!

The Exaltation of the Saints

In his references to his oneness with the Father, Jesus was describing the ultimate oneness that will exist between the Creator and the creation in the consummation of God's eternal purposes. Jesus was the firstborn. A first implies others still to come. His oneness with the Father was the same oneness in which all the saints now share partially and in which all will share like Jesus in a fuller way for all eternity. In this world we have been sprinkled with the Spirit. In the consummation of all things we will be totally immersed in those divinely refreshing, healing waters forever.

During Jesus' ministry, he was in union with the Spirit as the archetype, the pattern in which the saints are now in union with the Spirit. Like him, we are reconciled to God, sealed unto the great day of God's full revelation, by our baptism into the ever living Spirit of Christ.

The grand picture revealed in Scripture is that God will be fully manifested and expressed in his Heir. Christ is not just the man named Jesus who lived and died two thousand years ago. He is the living, corporate Lord inheriting all the fullness, all the power, and all the future of God himself (1 Cor. 15:23-28). Because of his faithfulness, he was given the Name above all names. He is the Son, the Inheritor of all that God is or will be. He is the One who is, who was, and who is to come, the Almighty (Rev. 1:8). And he is the Archetype of our salvation.

Wondrously, the Father is changing, from glory to glory. He is transferring all that pertains to himself unto the Son. God is in the process of creating a fabulous new world, a new city, a fantastic new Body in which to dwell forever. And wonder of all wonders, the saints will share in that glorious, towering Temple! They too will nobly carry the name of Christ and of God upon them. The saints will in fact compose this wondrous new Body of God, this living Temple!

The Son is not an only son. He is no longer the only-begotten. With him is every child of God who shares in Christ (John 17:21-23; Phil. 3:20-21; 1 John 3:1-2). We are co-inheritors with Jesus (Rom. 8:16-17). We, too, are God's Children and, like Jesus, inherit all the blessings of our heavenly Father, and his nature (John 1:12-13; 1 John 3:1-2). We share the same address. We live in the same House (John 14:1-3). Every Child of the Father will share joyously in the unimagined splendors that will be our shining glory at the coming Consummation. We eagerly await our transformation in anticipation and wonder.

The traditional doctrine of the Trinity would evict us from our new home. It tells us that we don't belong. It would raise up a flood of absurdities to drive us from our magnificent inheritance. But we have flood insurance. We're fully covered.

The Saints Are Called Gods (Ps. 82:1-8)

When Jesus called himself the Son of God, he was accused of blasphemy. But he reminded his accusers that the Scriptures themselves called those to whom the word of God came, Gods (John 10:30-36). The quote was from the Psalms (Ps. 82:1-8). That psalm says that God judges in the midst of the gods. God himself is quoted as saying that his children are gods (*Elohim*), sons of the Most High. Yet they will die like men.

God himself has spoken, and yet, incredibly, Trinitarian translators and commentators have no qualm about contradicting God himself. They try to explain away these verses by omitting capitalization and insisting that the "gods" are really only judges who acted for God (Exod. 21:6, 22:8-9). Do you recognize the term-switch here? Can you see the substitution? How the churches love that game! It's how the word of God is twisted to suit tradition.

But the judges who acted for God are not called gods. Jesus applies the title of divinity to those to whom the Gospel came. They are Gods and Sons of the Most High, he says. Jesus was hinting for his accusers that he was truly the Son of God, yet he would die according to Scripture like every human dies. And he implies that everyone who receives the Word of Christ will have the same destiny as his. They, too, will be called the Children of God. The

Scriptures cannot be broken. The saints' inheritance is secure. God has given his word on it.

The psalm does not say that God judges among the judges. He judges among the Gods. The Son will judge the world (John 6:22). The saints likewise will judge the world, sitting on the same throne, sharing in his divine authority and absolute power (1 Cor. 6:23; Rev. 3:21). It is the saints, not worldly judges, who are called Gods, and through whom God will judge the world. God is in their midst (Matt. 16:19, 18:18-20; 2 Cor. 5:19-20; Rev. 20:4).

Yes, God judges in their midst, and through them. In the Judgment, according to the pages of sacred Scripture, the saints will be seated on the great white throne of God with Christ. God will be in them, and they will be in God. And yet the saints will die like Christ Jesus and like every other human.

God's Oneness Is Composite

There is only one God. But his oneness is not simple. God's oneness is composite, like that of Adam and Eve (Gen. 2:24; Num. 13:23). God said that those two would become one (*echad*). And he used the very same word to describe his own oneness (Deut. 6:4). The pair primeval was made in his image and likeness. Their marriage imaged that of the Lamb with his Bride, who become one Body. The oneness of God is composite, and changing. He is becoming flesh. He is metamorphosing.

The Scriptures show that Father, Son, and Spirit are all three of them God. But it never says that these three have forever composed one God called the Trinity. And if God can be three, a Father, Son, and Spirit, all of whom are God, can he not be more? Why must we stop at three, if the Bible doesn't? God is composite.

He is Spirit, but he is also Flesh. To deny this is to deny his word, and rebelliously attempt to separate Christ and God, who are now and forever One.

Putting Limits on Grace and Mercy

The doctrine of the Trinity severely limits God's love and infinite mercy. In his unspeakable grace he has received us into the inner sanctum of the Godhead. God is no longer what he was. He is transferring all that pertains to him unto Christ. And Christ is a people. In him, God is growing a Body to serve him and do his bidding through the ages of the ages. That is the true Gospel, and the full revelation of God's purpose. There can be nothing more overwhelmingly glorious than the hope and expectation of swimming in this sublime splendor forever and ever with God, sharing the eternal future with him.

But the churches would brush aside this greatness of God's goodness and grace, to keep God forever above and beyond us. Their doctrine would reject God's will and purpose and substitute nonsense in its place. It would deny the truth of Calvary, and the reconciliation that Jesus accomplished. By promoting and insisting upon the false doctrine of the Trinity, the traditional churches have unwittingly denied the entire reconciling ministry of Christ. Whatever intrudes between God and his beloved to keep them separate is an abomination, and the object of God's wrath.

Once more, the Church has been caught in adultery, in the very act. She has created a three-headed image that keeps God and the redeemed separate. She has tried to clothe this indecency with Scripture. But the clothing is too small and does not fit, and exposes the shamefulness beneath. Turn away from it, child.

Unacceptable Worship

The invention of absurd falsehoods to describe God is not acceptable worship. The construction in words and traditions of a monster in order to praise it as if it were God, as the churches have done, is itself monstrous. It's a repetition of the ancient Baal worship by apostate Israel. The triune God of tradition is neither rational nor scriptural, nor true. The doctrine strikes at the very heart of Jesus' ministry, misunderstanding the Scriptures. God is not wholly other, nor immutable, nor illogically one yet three, nor forever unknowable. He will be completely revealed and known in Christ Jesus, who is inheriting all that pertains to God (Col. 1:19; Heb. 1:2). And Christ Jesus is not a mystery far beyond understanding.

Falsehoods are the Devil's work, always. It does not honor God when we ascribe absurdity to him with the excuse that, "if we could understand, it would not be God." If a notion is untrue, or absurd, it is not of God no matter how wonderful or fantastic it may seem. True worship does not make God into a three-headed absurdity. Lies can never describe the God of truth, or the truth of God. Like idols, lies have no reality. But truth is real. We worship a God of truth, and must speak only truth about him.

A Changing God

It is obvious that God changes, to everyone not blinded by the shroud of loyalty to tradition. Every movement in the creation changes the Creator's relation to it, and his knowledge of it. For God to remain unchanged, the world would have to remain forever unchanged too. Any movement in the creation absolutely necessitates a change in God. God is in the creation. And he moves within it. His Spirit was moving over the face of the deep in the beginning. And he was deeply involved in the beginning of the new creation when the divine Word became flesh. And it was a change. Creation itself is a change in God. Knowledge of change is itself a change too.

If God could know all things at once, as if there were no movement or procession, then he would not know real change. He would not know all things, then, What this means is that, if he knew all things, he couldn't know all things. It's like that old cliché, "I never say never." But history isn't a still picture for him. A photo of a bird in flight is not a bird in flight. Life is a movie, not a photograph. Even speaking takes time. You can't say a word in an instant. And the Bible says that God speaks. In fact, knowledge itself is a process of change. Experience occurs over time. If God knows change, then he has experienced it. He has changed. An unchanging God could not know anything, even with three heads. An unchanging God could not create. It would change him.

God's Inquiries

As a figure looking forward to Christ and the End-times, God presented himself to the patriarch Abraham as lacking full knowledge of the sinfulness of Sodom and Gomorrah. He had come down to investigate (Gen. 18:21). He was there to see if what he had heard about the place was true. He wanted to be merciful, and if he would find at least ten righteous men there, he would not destroy the whole city. He showed himself to be adaptable and changeable, and willing to overlook much. In this episode God was purposely prefiguring the events of the last days that would lead to Har-Magedon, when he would come down again to visit Babylon. Sodom and Gomorrah are a symbol for the last days.

Importantly, God admitted that he did not know experientially the reality of Abraham's faithfulness until Abraham demonstrated it. It required a test (Gen. 22:12). This gives evidence that Abraham was free too. He was not a robot. He could have chosen to be unfaithful. His faith was expressed and made complete as it was demonstrated (Jas. 2:22). And the patriarch's faithfulness in freedom affected God. He responded favorably to Abraham's faith.

God led Israel in the wilderness for the same reason, to test them (Deut. 8:2, 13:3). Their experience provided God with experiential knowledge about the true condition of their heart. Israel was not a host of robots on the march.

To Move and Be Moved

If he knew all things perfectly in advance, he could not newly influence the creation at all. Everything that would ever happen would be known and shown already in God's mind. He could never know something that would later be untrue. He could not know a fact that was not a fact. Nothing new could ever occur. He could not change the picture. God could do nothing but stare, paralyzed, at the test pattern on his TV, unable to reach over and press the remote control or change the channel. It would all be set in stone in the Creator's mind.

God is here in the creation with us. He is not just pressing his nose against the window, wishing he could come inside. And in the creation, things move and change. The Spirit moves within the world. God is not outside of time and space. He lives in eternity, which is time without limits. But our own days are included in the same forever. Eternity is not a separate world outside of time. It's a cruise down the open highway of reality, the wind blowing in our face, and no stop signs. Change happens. It's the primordial fact of existence. And God is here beside us, the wind in his face too. He's driving.

No Unmoving Center

No, Aristotle, there's no immutable God. A Mover cannot remain unmoving, or unmoved. There is no unmoving core, no infinitely small point at the center of the wheel of nature. The world ever rolls on the highway of newness and transformation. Change is everywhere. It's the very character and essence of existence, and of life. It's the nature of reality itself. And God is immensely alive. He is life itself, the very Fount of newness and change. Change is the essence of God's being, of who God is. He is the Creator. History is the expression of his creativity. He makes what happens to happen. He speaks, and it becomes. And he wants to drive off into the future with us. He wants company on the road.

No Unchanging God

When the Bible speaks of God unchanging, it's not talking about his nature. It's talking about his unswerving intention for the creation (Num. 23:19; 1 Sam. 15:29). The Gospel of our hope and security rests firmly on the solid bedrock of God's purpose (Heb. 6:17-18, 7:21; Jas 1:17). He's not going to leave his project half done. He'll finish it. His unchanging will is to accomplish the fullness of all things in the fullness of the Son and Heir (Heb. 13:8). God has died, and now his will must go into effect (Heb. 9:17). The Heirs will receive their portions as his testament is read. And its reading will bring its realization.

In the book of Hebrews, Jesus is said to be unchanging too (Heb. 1:12). But clearly, he changes. And his very sharing in God is a change in the Creator. God has put on flesh, in the Incarnation and in the cross event. This verse does not mean that God remains forever unchanged. That would be absurd, and contradict the whole Bible. It means that he remains in existence. He exists always. Literally, the psalm quoted in Hebrews says that the earth and heavens will be changed like a garment, "but you are he" (Ps. 102:27). It does not say that God is immutable, but rather that God lives forever. And besides, an unchanging God would be a denial of the Trinity, as well as of Christ Jesus.

It hints of our eternal life. Because God lives eternally, because he remains and his purpose continues, we too shall live eternally as we share in him. God's faithfulness and power are the solid ground of our security. His Word of power is the very expression of himself, which is life without limits, of creativity freed from bondage. Death cannot destroy him. Change is the very expression of his creative nature. It's what he does. It's who he is. He is re-creating himself, metamorphosing into Christ's fullness.

God's Intention to Travel

God isn't homebound. He wants to put on his new clothes and go, go, go (Ps. 102:26-27; Heb. 1:12). He wants to get behind the wheel of the new creation and let'r rip down the open highway. He wants to see new things, experience new sights and sounds. He wants to go places. Creation will occur as God expresses himself. And it will be in and through the saints! The unchanging will of God is to experience newness and change. And he himself is the Cause and composition of it, the Creator. Creation is change.

This world originated from him. It was a change in his existence. It will return to him, washed and polished, and ready to roll. The creation is the expression of God. And his alphabet is without number, his vocabulary unlimited. God is free.

Jesus has been exalted fully into oneness with the Creator, eternally. God has changed! He has received Christ unto himself. Soon every saint will participate in that same oneness. God is growing for himself a Body. *He is not an aloof Trinity, but a gracious and involved Multiplicity, a Plurality.* He is a loving, connecting Creator. He reaches out beneficently and draws his creation unto himself. Together they will go on a honeymoon journey of never ending newness and ever evolving creativity, for he is the Creator.

Chapter SIX

The Gospel of Glory

God's Loving Call

Because God has prepared this astounding destiny of never-ending blessedness and bliss for his Children, he has left us clues to guide us and to encourage us. He wants our faith to grow, for faith sets in motion the unopposable power of creation. The prayer of faith is an inkling of the stupendous power that will be available to the saints in Christ. It's a hint of our coming glory. Our authority over all the power of the enemy in this world is a promise.

This world waves to get our attention, and then points to Christ (Ps. 19:1-6, Acts 14:16-17, 17:24-28). As in Eden, God calls to us in the cool breezes of the day, in the gusting winds of history (Gen. 3:8). These softly blowing billows caress our face and urge us to join him in the dance of creation that whirls all around us and fills the air with the music of promise. As we watch, his fluent Word turns the pages of history and expresses God's will into reality. The melodies of his voice that float in the breezes invite us to dazzling scenes of unimpeded light. We must pull ourselves free, then, from the scratching, clinging forest of tradition and step out onto the unobstructed vistas of eternity, into the unfettered glories God has prepared for us. This is the creation's message. It's the Gospel message, a strong and powerful word of life. The creation is a harbinger of things ever more marvelous. From the beginning, the world has flowed with the unstinted promises of God.

Preparing for the Light

From the beginning, the creation has hinted of the Gospel of holiness, of separation. Early in the bleak, beclouded world was God's mighty Word, speaking order and purpose into the formless and empty void. This utterly potent Word of God created the light, and God saw that it was good. And he separated it from the darkness. Then he spoke again, and there appeared an expanse in the heavens to separate the waters above from those below. And it was good, so he commanded the waters below to separate and the dry land to emerge, and it happened. His Word has ever been a sword of separation, a call toward holiness, and then more holiness.

At his creative Word, humans arose from the earth, and were temporarily separated too, but complementary, male and female. They were naked, needing to be clothed, hinting of the future, reflecting God's long-range plans and purposes for the creation and for himself. They whispered of the world's present separation from him, and its future return in washed, renewed splendor. They imaged God.

Later, he chose Noah as a herald of things to come. He separated him out from the press of humanity, to portray the coming One who would save his family from the watery deep of death and extinction. They would enter into a crisp and clean, freshly washed new world of wonder and open skies. Still later he chose Abraham, calling him his friend, separating him from his country and people, promising to bless all the families of the earth through his coming Seed. He chose the line of Israel then, a people separated from the nations by his holy presence among them and by the Law that spoke of the coming One. He sent kings and prophets, figures of the coming Lord, ever urging Israel to be holy and separate from this suffocating world of everyday living. God has ever whispered to humanity, "not this world, but the next."

After all these many preparations, he sent his Son into the world, to gather up all the creation as a Bridegroom gathers his bride into his arms. God's dealings with humans in history have ever teemed with hints of Christ in his reconciling, sanctifying grandeur and glory.

With Christ's coming, God's purpose was displayed openly. The former hints and whispers became loud voices, and shouts of victory! God no longer merely intimates (Heb. 1:1-3). Parables and allusions have removed their masks (John 16:25-30). The word is becoming clearer, the firmament in the new creation is lightening. As the darkness in the expanse of heaven clears, it reveals the divine Sun, moon, and stars. The light of God's glory is being manifested ever more brightly in the face of Christ (2 Cor. 4:6). God is removing the veil from his face!

Avoiding the Light

But, like the face of Moses, the divine light is too bright for the world (Exod. 34:29-35; 2 Cor. 3:12-18, 4:4-6). It runs to the dark and hides, for its deeds are evil (John 3:19-21). Aaron has once more made a molten image for the people to worship in the place of God. True to the foreshadowing pattern, the leaders of Christianity have formed a golden calf and placed it in the church sanctuary. In the place of an involved, concerned Father, they have set up an unchanging, unmoving idol, and given it three heads. For the God of grace and mercy they have substituted a monstrosity of fiendish tortures and hellish punishments.

The many stripes and flavors of Christianity are all of them guilty. From the crowd of churches a raucous din of blasphemies rises to high heaven. For God's rest many substitute Sunday. Others walk up brazenly to the cross and there, standing at that altar of pure, limitless love, shake their finger in God's face and denounce him as a conniving deceiver, as a traitor who abandoned his own son.

Jesus offers more than closeness and intimacy. He offers literal oneness with God. But the churches say not so, insisting that God is forever pure Spirit, supremely holy and apart from the world and humanity. He exists far beyond our puny understanding and comprehension, they insist, as if they understood him. To honor their idol they unwittingly deny Christ Jesus and the Gospel. They forget that Jesus is God in the flesh. God has a Body. And yet, for the churches reconciliation has become mere metaphor.

In the place of Christ, many churches substitute their own vicarious, adulterous self, and invite allegiance. To be joined to Christ people must be joined to their church, they claim. Such a church has become a substitute for Christ, who is himself described as a substitute for humanity, a substitute substituting for a substitute. Falsehood is piled upon falsehood.

With switched terms and subtle substitutions, they have cast a somber pall over the Gospel of glory. Once clothed with the Sun, the Church has soiled and torn her garments and now stumbles about wretched and naked. Brazenly, she has tied the blindfold of make-believe around the peoples' eyes lest they see her shame. Babylon is utterly fallen. Turn away, child. And do not shed any tears.

The New Beginning

We must stop trying to hide from God among the fruitless trees of tradition. Our eyes have been opened, and we have been clothed with Christ (Gen. 3:21). We must leave behind, then, the shadows of the forest, and step boldly out onto the verdant, flowered mountain slopes of salvation. We must gaze again, wide-eyed and in wonderment, upon the sunrise and sunset of this creation, and recognize that this vast panorama is finally just a preview. A new day is rising over the mountains.

Salvation and entrance into heaven are not the end of life. They're its first, unsteady steps. Salvation is an invitation to walk in the Spirit, and to run, and to fly! This world is a prelude. The end of this world is the beginning of the next one. Sunset and evening of this present creation promise a new morning. The golden dawn will bring the start of an everlasting journey of creativeness shared between the Creator and the saints.

Saved and exalted humanity is the end product of the slow, patient process by which God has been carefully preparing a Bride for himself. When Adam and Eve came on the earthly scene, God chose them to be ancestors of Christ. They were the progenitors of the race that would one day give birth to the Son and Heir of God. In him, God relinquishes all things, in order to fulfill all things. In the Son of Man, God will live the life of eternal newness that is his future. And we are included in him.

This present world was never God's ultimate objective. It was just a first step on the journey to Christ, and he has never stopped to rest. God is never lazy and inactive. His nature is to exist, to be, to live. And life is movement and growth. The living God is not a scowling statue of stone, motionless and unchanging. He is ceaselessly dynamic and endlessly creative, the very essence of innovation and change. God is perpetual motion.

The goal of creation is newness, not stasis and stagnancy. The river of history will not end in a stagnant pool. The uttermost heights of bliss, the beatific visions of God's Shekinah splendor, are not the sight of an unmoving idol. God is not a couch potato. Nor is he a golden gargoyle with three heads, immutable and eternally transfixed upon its base. He is the Creator. And creation means movement and change. As God expresses himself reality is transformed, and newness develops. Creation's future is a never-ending journey of originality and quest upon which the Creator will take the transformed and glorified saints after the consummation. They will serve him forever, blissfully, love answering to love unendingly as they create together the exciting adventures of eternity.

A Joyful Response

We must, then, learn to live now the life that is our future. Our destiny begins with the first steps of faith, learning to let God's power flow through us and give us daily the joyous shout of victory in Christ. He is even now becoming the expression of our being. With his Holy Spirit within us, we are becoming the embodiment and expression of the Creator! His Word has become incarnate in us. As we experience his will and express that will in our daily walk and talk, God's overwhelming Word of creative power, indeed his very self, is expressed in us and through us.

We have this Spirit of life, this Word of God, in seed form now, planted in earthen vessels. It will take root and grow. Its blossoms will fill heaven's air with the perfume of God's glories for all eternity. Our lives of prayer and praise are censers of sweet incense, our service of worship, and the exciting story unto which the Bible calls us. We must not only read it, we must enter its pages. We have important, satisfying roles to play in the ongoing story of life. We must become living words of God, joyful songs of praise.

God has made us with freedom to respond to his gentle call. The freedom in which we develop here in this time is an inkling of our future with God in Christ. We must practice our purpose, and prepare for eternity. We must turn our gaze upward and outward to ever larger vistas, greater expanses, for we will soon be experiencing creative life together as One with God forever and ever. This is God's unchanging will and our certain destiny. We have the assurance of its reality in the creation of this world, in the history of God's dealings with humanity, and in our personal experience of Christ within us.

This is what it's all about. This is the reason and goal of salvation. We will worship God by serving him forever and ever as we share fully in the divine life of the Creator unendingly, for as long as eternity rolls. How awesome and majestic is our God!

Yes, we will take part in telling the ongoing story of reality itself. Existence will be ours to name. Human speech is a hint of marvels yet unimagined. It is an inkling of our coming creative life together with God. In a true sense, we will be speaking for God, as he speaks in us. We must learn to let his word flow from our lips. We are his witnesses, his mouthpiece. And his Word is ever creative. It gives form to reality.

His Word is the expression of himself, and he is the Ground of all being, the Cause of it all, the Creator. We have the gift of speech and the power of his Word in order to prepare for our incredible future in Christ.

Learning to Live

Salvation, then, is not about following rules that stifle, bind, and enslave. The Gospel of glory is about learning to live in the service of God, gliding high and unhindered on the gentle breezes of the Spirit. We are learning to take hold of life as it will be in the coming age, creative and free. Christ has made us lords and masters of this world and the next. We are the true master race, we who belong to Christ and who hold eternity in our hearts. Even the winds and the waves will obey us, as we walk in Christ. The principalities and powers that now hold us fast will submit meekly to our control. We will command them with the power and authority of the Creator himself, and they will obey.

His desire is that we arise and walk in the joy-filled freedom of the Spirit. Soon we will run and not grow weary, just as he promised. Indeed, we will sprout wings and soar high and unrestrained like eagles in the open expanses of God's own freedom. This is our certain destiny, and it will be glorious far beyond any of our present musings.

We have within us the same Word that created this world, alive and bristling with untiring energy and dynamism. This divine Word of power still speaks and pierces the gloom. The Spirit is moving over the face of the present waters, fluttering within our hearts and minds, flying from our lips. Even as we speak, the cherubim of glory flash like lightning over the restless deep. They thunder with God's omnipotent Word of newness and creativity, once more calling forth the light, scattering the darkness to reveal the bright, multicolored new world of God's supreme, unlimited sovereignty (Rev. 4:5, 8:5). And the coming new world is good, very, very good. O, that he would open our eyes, like Gehazi, to see the glories that surround us (2 Kgs. 6:17)!

God earnestly desires and intends that we fulfill this our exhilarating destiny. So he lives and moves within us, becoming the stunning reality of that destiny. He surrounds us and encloses us in himself. Then he speaks within us, softly, patiently, guiding and empowering our lives. It pleases him when we listen to his melodious voice, and understand, and repeat for others what he says. It brings him intense joy when we walk the windswept path that the Spirit clears for us, and learn daily to accomplish his sovereign and sublime purposes. It brings him great satisfaction.

As we walk in his will, fulfilling his desires, God is honored and glorified. As we gratefully serve him in freedom, our lives emit the sweet, fragrant incense of worship. They become fervent prayers and hymns of praise, glad offerings to God in concert with countless angels and the whole creation.

It is our sublime destiny and supreme joy to sing with our lives blessing, honor, glory, and dominion forever and ever to Him who sits upon the throne. This grateful service to God is the exhilarating reason of our existence. It is the true and highest worship, and the fulfillment of the Creator's purposes. The glory and majesty of God lives in the life-praises of his people.

So then, the churches have gotten it all wrong. The creation came from the very substance of God, not from nothingness. It will be reconstituted into a new, glorified Body in which God will dwell to pursue his ever burning future. To that purpose he has intentionally and carefully nudged human history at key points so that in due time Jesus would be born, fully human and mortal, in order to draw the creation back to its Creator. Jesus began the process of reconciliation by first receiving oneness with God through Spirit baptism, and then by taking flight bodily back to God through the cross and resurrection. And gloriously, he is our great Example!

Like Jesus, those who receive the Son receive the Father, and are reconciled with God in the same manner as was Jesus, to share the same throne, co-heirs of God with Christ. Those who never receive the Son do not have eternal life. But neither do they receive unending torture. There will be no Hell of eternal torments, no Purgatory, no Limbo in our ever-coursing future. There will be only God's goodness flowing throughout heaven.

Nor is God a three-headed aberration, a gargoyle, an eternal Trinity. He is infinitely more. He is the Creator, the all-powerful One who is making all things new, and saving everyone everywhere who receives him. Like Jesus the firstfruits, every saint shares fully in the developing, growing Body of God. Every saint receives divinity, and Oneness within the Godhead. In Christ, the creation is being formed into the very Temple of God. The creation's wondrous destiny is to be, through the saints, the helpmeet of the Creator!

That is the true and immensely moving meaning of the Incarnation. It was not a one-time event, nor was it limited to only one human. The same destiny is available to anyone with ears to hear. God is calling to whoever will come, to drink deeply from the refreshing waters of life, his own life. God is metamorphosing, and inviting humans to metamorphose with him. He is inviting them to die like him, in order to live like him. That is the true and astoundingly glorious Gospel of eternal life. Creator and creation are coming together again. Believe it, child. The glad reunion is coming soon. Are you ready?

CPSIA information can be obtained at www.ICGtesting.com
Printed in the USA
LVOW12s0249150414

381677LV00001B/2/P